FINDING MIDDLE GROUND in K-12 Education

Balancing Best Practices and the Law

A resource for teachers, principals, superintendents, and school boards

Jim Burgett

Brian D. Schwartz

 For information, contact Education Communication Unlimited, P.O. Box 845, Novato, CA 94948 / (800) 563-1454 / www.middlegroundforeducators.com.

First printing,
June 2009

▶Cover Design by Douglas Burgett
▶Proofreading by Sharon Rinderer

ISBN 978-0-9796295-6-3

Also available in .PDF format: ISBN 978-09796295-7-0

Table of Contents

Legal Disclaimer

The ideas, suggestions, and advice provided in this book are those of the authors. While every effort has been made to present sound and accurate legal and practical guidance, the information herein is not warranted and does not constitute legal advice. The reader should be aware that the field of education law is in a constant state of change. Additionally, the facts in specific situations and the laws of certain jurisdictions may change the recommendations and suggestions rendered herein. Readers are strongly encouraged to check with private legal counsel before undertaking any decision that may require legal guidance or implementing or adopting any policy, procedure, or practice.

Dedications

◆ I am blessed through family. It all starts with a wonderful wife, three kids that make my wife and me prouder than we can share, and six (to date) grandkids that are all very special. Yet this book is dedicated to my in-laws, who round off the blessing of our family. Our two sons-in-law, Mike and Brian, and our daughter-in-law Vanessa are exceptional in every way. They make our lives richer and fuller. They are faithful in their spiritual lives and faithful to their families. Each one exhibits a great work ethic and each adds much to provide a peaceful and loving family. This book was a work of love, written as a cooperative effort with the intent of making this a better world. And those same descriptors are the reason I am dedicating this book to Mike, Brian, and Vanessa.

Jim Burgett

◆ This book is dedicated to my wife, Jennifer Schwartz, who has provided me with much of the material herein. It is also dedicated to John Ourth (1941-2007), a teacher and mentor who is dearly missed.

Brian Schwartz

“Education is the most powerful weapon you can use to change the world.”

Nelson Mandela

Introduction

Being a teacher, administrator, board member, school employee, parent, or even a student is tricky business these days. Never before have there been so many issues to contend with.

Today there are more laws, more rules, more regulations, more mandates, and more pressures. Equally as perplexing, it seems that these days the art of discussing an issue has been replaced with formal negotiations, legal intervention, and threats of third-party involvement. It also seems that schoolhouse discipline is more often at odds with home discipline, and that some families resent or reject the old concept that the school is, in fact, entitled to act in place of the parent.

It also seems that technology, media, the Internet, and things such as "MySpace" have made life more confusing and conflicting. Only a few years ago kids would be happy to sneak a peak at *Playboy*, whereas today hard core porn is widely obtained at disgustingly young ages. And it is well documented that girls mature at a younger age than they used to, while boys mature later, confusing established and traditional expectations. No wonder parents struggle with control and discipline and schools are conflicted in their roles as well.

We all know that the rights and obligations of anyone and everyone, and the protection of those rights and obligations, make education more legal and litigious than at any time in history. And it's not just the schools. One only needs think of the "HIPAA" rules in hospitals that prevent even members of families from learning why someone was admitted or what is happening. Or how about the plethora of mailings and information sent to everyone who has a credit card or business account that outlines the privacy acts, rate changes, and other legal minutia that we would guess few ever read. It seems we have all gone a bit crazy covering our proverbial rear ends at the cost of common sense and simple talk.

So when two exceptional warriors on today's educational battlefield—who have worked together for many years, each in differing roles but both working to improve our schools for kids and everyone else involved—agreed to share their experience and thoughts on paper, to add some light to this half-legal, half common sense mayhem, we jumped at the possibility of sharing their thoughts with you!

But what to call this much needed book? The term "middle ground" kept reappearing, as a place where the best of all actions and results might be found. So we decided to focus on how education leaders can, through their actions, help us define "Middle Ground" as a place rather than a concept. A place where two (or more) sides can come together and solve problems without going ballistic, without unnecessary craziness, rather with some sense of balance and resolution.

We want to look at the two elements of solving problems: the practical side and the legal side. Neither can be consistently successful by itself. Ignore the legal ramifications of most issues and you walk on thin ice. This ice may break and you drop quickly into cold and costly water. Ignore the common sense of resolving a conflict and there is a good chance that you will do it at the cost of sound and positive relationships. You may win the lawsuit but in the long term lose the game. So Middle Ground is our collective goal on these pages—common sense resolutions based on sound legal thinking and advice—brought by two veterans well trained in the groves of resolution.

As a retired superintendent and an educator who has been going to schools for 58 years (starting in kindergarten), Jim Burgett has proven to be a sensible leader and a trusted mentor for many educators. He has always maintained a philosophy of working with school attorneys, getting their direction, advice, and input. He selected lawyers who were more eager to find common sense resolutions than encourage legal action. He depended on their wisdom and expertise.

In addition, you know Jim as the author of *Teachers Change Lives 24/7*, as well as the co-author, with Drs. Jim Rosborg and Max McGee, of *What Every Superintendent and Principal Needs to Know* and *The Perfect School.*

Brian Schwartz is an education lawyer and an excellent communicator. He is an author (of *The Law of Homeschooling)* and a speaker who presents his thoughts and legal advice in English, not legalese. Well respected by educators throughout the United States, he has emerged as one of the most trusted lawyers in the profession.

They have found the Middle Ground in writing this book. The format is simple. Each chapter contains a comprehensive overview of a specific topic, followed by one or several case studies reflecting actual situations (altered to protect the parties involved). Once a case study is presented, Jim will share some resolution strategies and Brian will give his ideas, suggestions, warnings, and legal concerns. Then the two authors help the reader think through situations in search of that Middle Ground.

This is not a template for legal advice or educational strategies. Nor is this book intended to be a set of legal guidelines or a textbook on management. It is a tool to help teachers, administrators, parents, and others associated with schools think through complex and difficult situations. The purpose is to give assistance to those who want to do a better job of recognizing legal concerns and managing successfully. It is written in a simple, conversational tone, but with the intent of providing inspiration and guidance to make schools a better place for kids and a good place to work and learn.

We don't expect you to agree with their opinions in every case. And, of course, we all know that there are other, valid opinions and suggestions, too.

Here are Jim and Brian's best thoughts, plus the concept of seeking a Middle Ground to draw from the legal and practical the very best resolutions to keep the school systems safe, sane, solvent, and their primary attention on the very best ways of educating today's kids—tomorrow's leaders

Welcome to the Middle Ground!

Gordon Burgett
Publisher, Education Communication Unlimited

Chapter One

How to Keep Yourself Legally Safe: Does This Suit Make Me Look Bad?

Brian D. Schwartz

Introduction

In today's litigious society, not surprisingly, there has been an increase in lawsuits brought against teachers, administrators, and school board members. So much so, that it seems every newborn child is now provided with a birth certificate, social security number, cell phone (more on that later), and a lawyer. Although anyone who wants to file a lawsuit and is able to find the courthouse can sue you, the main purpose of this chapter is to assure that defending these lawsuits is the burden and responsibility of the local school district and not teachers, administrators, and school board members personally.

Unfortunately, we are aware of several situations where individual school employees have been held personally liable when sued for actions (or inactions) they thought were taken in the course and scope of their employment. In these cases, the employee has been forced to pay for damages and, sometimes, legal fees out of his or her own pocket. To fully appreciate the scope of this problem, it is helpful to understand the basic anatomy of a lawsuit.

When a student is emotionally or physically injured, parents can file a lawsuit in the name of their child. (A parent or guardian must actually file the lawsuit in cases where the child is a minor and therefore cannot sue in his or her own name.) When the lawsuit is filed, it is a standard legal practice to name as defendants all parties who may have had an involvement in the situation. For example, if a student falls off the school's monkey bars and breaks his arm, the ensuing lawsuit may include as defendants the teacher, who was responsible for the supervision of the child; the principal, who developed the supervision plan; the superintendent, as the chief executive officer of the district, and members of the school board, who are ultimately obligated (in most states) to make policy decisions.

Not only are the above parties the frequent targets of litigation, each can also be sued in their official capacity and/or their individual capacity. Allegations of wrongdoing that are made within the course and scope of the school employee or board member's duties are generally said to have happened in the person's official capacity. Allegations of wrongdoing that occur outside one's official duties are said to have happened in the person's individual capacity.

Again, in terms of an example, let us assume that a physical education class is engaged in a game of "dodge ball." (Most of us can remember when this was an acceptable educational practice.) Let's further assume that the physical education teacher decides to participate in the game, and as a direct result of his participation, a student is injured. Here, the parents might sue the teacher in both his official and individual capacities. Although the teacher was teaching and supervising at the time, thereby acting in his official capacity, he was also playing with the children, which goes beyond the scope of his job duties and allows the teacher to be sued in his individual capacity as well.

It is important to distinguish between allegations brought against individuals in their official capacity versus their individual capacity because this distinction frequently governs who pays the costs of the lawsuit and any resulting damages. When a lawsuit is filed alleging only that an employee or board member acted in his or her official capacity, the school district is generally obligated to provide representation to the individual and pay any and all damages that may result. If the interests of the employee are not coextensive with the interests of the school district, the employee can usually request that the district pay for a separate attorney for the employee, instead of having the district's attorney represent both parties.

When a lawsuit includes allegations that the employee or board member acted in his or her individual capacity, there is an issue as to whether the school district must represent the individual. In many cases, the school district will initially assume representation of the employee or board member, but reserve the right to end representation if a judge or jury eventually determines that the employee or board member failed to act within the course and scope of his or her duties. When this happens, the employee or board member is generally not required to reimburse the school district for the cost of his or her defense, but the employee or board member must personally pay all damages and other costs imposed by the court.

Additionally, it is important to note that a school district can, on its own motion, seek to withdraw its representation of the employee or school board member because the district believes that the individual acted outside the scope of his or her duties, regardless of how the lawsuit is filed. Likewise, an employee or board member can sue to force the school district to provide representation in cases where the individual is sued in his or her individual capacity, but believes that all actions were taken in the course and scope of employment.

In most cases, however, the school district, employee, board member, and other defendants have similar interests—mainly to get the lawsuit dismissed for lack of wrongdoing—

and the school district's legal team can represent all defendants. However, if an individual employee or school board member ever feels that his or her interests are not fully represented, then the employee or board member should petition the district in writing for the appointment of separate counsel.

Again, under the theory that anyone can file a lawsuit, the aim of this chapter is to help school employees and school board members protect themselves, so that any lawsuit is handled at the school district's expense and not at the individual's expense. It is therefore important to explore in greater depth what it means for a school employee or board member to have acted within the course and scope of his or her duties. Generally speaking, employees and school board members act within the course and scope of their duties if they are (1) performing only tasks they are paid or legally obligated to do and (2) performing these functions in a reasonable manner.

In light of the above test, it is extremely important that school employees and board members know the exact requirements of their jobs. For teachers and administrators, job duties are found in places such as school and district policy manuals, collective bargaining agreements, contracts, and state statutes. For board members, job functions are generally a matter of state law.

If a school employee ever has a question as to whether a certain function falls within his or her job duties, it is important to seek the approval of a supervisor. For example, let's assume that a teacher is driving to school one cold and snowy day and sees a young student who has missed her bus. The student is attempting to walk to school but the snow and wind are quickly turning her into a snowperson. Most of us (I hope) would not simply wave as we drove by, but would want to help the student get to school. However, after reading the above paragraphs, you should be asking yourself if transporting the student to school falls within your job duties. Since most teachers are not bus drivers, this question deserves serious consideration.

With these cold, hard facts (no pun intended), the teacher has a choice to make. Leave the student to her own means, hoping that she does not freeze to death, or pick up the student and risk being held personally liable if the student is somehow injured in the course of the teacher transporting her to school. In looking at this situation, there is Middle Ground. Since most of us have cell phones (if you don't, you can generally borrow one from the student), the teacher could place a call to the school and seek the permission from the principal or superintendent to bring the student to school. If this permission is granted, then transporting the student becomes a *de facto* job duty of the teacher, and she is covered legally if the student is injured on the way to school.

Now, a principal or superintendent who has just read the above scenario might ask if he is now on the hook personally if the student is injured. The answer is probably not. Most principals and superintendents are required, by law, policy, or practice to make these types of decisions, and such decisions therefore fall within their job function.

In looking at the second part of what it means to stay within the course and scope of one's duties, a school employee or board member must act reasonably. This means that an individual must act as a reasonable person would in his or her position under the circumstances. For example, a teacher is held to the standard of a reasonable teacher, a coach to the standard of a reasonable coach, an administrator to the standard of a reasonable administrator, and so forth.

What Jim and I have found is that most teachers, administrators, and school board members are reasonable people and act accordingly. Perhaps the one area where the reasonableness of teacher or administrator conduct has been challenged the most is that of intervening in a fight between students. In looking at teachers in particular, some are comfortable getting between two students who are fighting, while others are not. Here, either approach can be reasonable if addressed properly.

If a teacher does attempt to physically break up a student fight, the teacher should use no more force than is necessary to address the situation. Once the students are separated and the situation is abated from a safety standpoint, the teacher should refrain from making further physical contact with the students. In cases where the teacher, for his or her own safety, does not believe it prudent to step in the middle of the fight, acting reasonable involves directing the students to stop fighting and calling for assistance.

Building administrators, on the other hand, are probably held to a somewhat different standard when it comes to separating students who are fighting. Although a building administrator is not required to place him or herself in a dangerous situation, administrators are ultimately responsible for the safety of all students in the building. Hence, what it means to act reasonably probably requires the building administrator to be more proactive in handling the situation.

Again, it should be stressed that school employees who act reasonably under the circumstances and who perform only those job functions that they are hired or assigned to do should be indemnified and held harmless if they are ever sued. However, as discussed above, questions can sometimes arise as to whether or not an employee acted within the course and scope of his or her duties and therefore whether or not the school district is responsible for the employee's defense. To protect against this occurrence, we strongly recommend that teachers and administrators carry a personal malpractice-type insurance policy. This type of policy, which can be purchased through your insurance agent, will generally step in and provide coverage when there is an issue over whether or not the school district is responsible for representing and indemnifying the employee.

At this point, the reader may be wondering just how a school district goes about defending itself, its board members, and its employees against lawsuits. Defending against a lawsuit is an expensive and time-consuming proposition. Even if the district is successful, it can often take years and cost hundreds of thousands of dollars to resolve the situation.

School districts are deemed by many to have "deep pockets" and are therefore a frequent target of lawsuits. Because these institutions are funded with taxpayer money, most every state has put safeguards in place to protect school districts when defending against frivolous or meritless lawsuits. For lawsuits brought in tort (or brought for physical or emotional injuries), states have adopted tort immunity statutes. These laws, in part, reduce the exposure and liability of school employees, school board members, and school districts for acts and decisions that are made within the regular course of educating and providing for students.

Take, for example, a relatively recent case in Illinois where a student was injured after a car crash. The student was a new driver and asked the principal if he could leave school early due to deteriorating winter weather conditions. The principal refused the student's request and sent him back to class. When school was eventually dismissed at its regular time, the weather had caused extremely hazardous driving conditions and the student was involved in a personal injury crash on the way home from school. The student's parents instituted a lawsuit (remember anyone can sue you), but the Illinois Supreme Court eventually dismissed the suit based on a provision in the State's tort immunity act that protects employees from liability for discretionary decisions made in the scope of their employment. The Court reasoned that the principal had made a discretionary decision that the school board had authorized him to make and he was therefore protected under the State's tort immunity laws. The lawsuit against the school district was dismissed under another provision of the State law providing that if an employee is not liable, a school district cannot be held liable.

Imagine the chaos that would result if school employees and officials could be sued every time they made a decision that someone didn't like or indirectly caused damages. First, courts would be tied up doing nothing but litigating these cases. Second, and perhaps more important, the cost of litigating these lawsuits would cause taxes to escalate at an alarming rate. Some lawsuits, however, cannot be dismissed under tort immunity and must proceed through the court system. These cases serve the important function of helping us conclude where the line should be drawn in deciding what constitutes acceptable conduct for school employees and officials.

What we have done in each chapter is set out case studies that might happen (or have happened) to a school district or school employee. We will take turns addressing the situation from both a legal and practical perspective. In doing this, we hope to assist you, the reader, in handling situations that you may face in your daily interactions with parents, students and the community and be able to react in a way that is politically, professionally, ethically, and legally correct. We call that Middle Ground.

Case Study #1: Coach Hockets and the Stranded Student

Randy Hockets is coach of the freshman high school girls' basketball team. One night the team bus returns to the school parking lot after a game at a neighboring school district. Mr. Hockets is about to get in his car and leave, when he notices that one of the students, Amy Kneedcar, does not have a ride home. The student cannot contact her parents and begins to cry. It is almost 11:00 p.m. and Mr. Hockets does not want to leave the student alone, but is leery about giving her a ride home. Unfortunately, Miss Evans, the assistant coach, did not attend the game and Randy is the only school staff member around.

Legal Perspective:

This is a scenario that many a coach has experienced. The team bus returns late in the evening and one of the students is unable to get a ride home. This situation has been somewhat mitigated by the availability of cell phones, but this still happens on a fairly routine basis. I think the first reaction of most coaches (and most people in general) would be to drive the student home. However, from a legal perspective, this is a risky proposition for two primary reasons.

First, it is never recommended that a coach, teacher, administrator, or school employee put himself or herself in the situation of being alone with a student, especially in a vehicle. There have been several cases where students have made allegations of inappropriate conduct against a school employee. These allegations often take the form of sexual or physical abuse. Even though many of these allegations are without merit, it is very difficult to defend a school employee in cases where there are no witnesses and the complainant is a minor. The problem is compounded when the situation is alleged to have happened late at night. Even if the employee can be successfully defended against the allegations, the perception of wrongdoing is likely to stay with the employee for a long time to come.

Second, if the coach were to be involved in an accident while transporting the student, it is questionable whether the school district would be obligated to defend the coach in any ensuing lawsuit. Generally, school districts are required to indemnify and hold harmless employees who are sued for actions taken in the course and scope of their duties. In this case, it could be argued by the school district that driving the student home was outside the coach's duties, and therefore the school district does not have the obligation to provide the coach with a legal defense or pay any damages.

It should be clear from the above discussion that the coach should not drive the student home. I hope it is equally clear that the coach should not leave the crying student alone to fend for herself, no matter what the age of the student. The question therefore becomes: What should the coach do in this situation to assure that the student gets home? For thoughts on this matter, I turn to Jim.

Administrative Perspective:

You're right, Brian; this is a frequent problem. In the days before electricity, when I was actually a coach myself, I had this same situation. We didn't have cell phones back then, and it was not always possible to even get to a pay phone in some circumstances. And, to make matters even worse, it was usually cold, rainy, and miserable, and the kid lived 47 miles out in the middle of nowhere. Well, maybe not 47 miles, but you get the point.

What to do? Well, to begin with, preventive medicine often keeps aches and pains away, and in this case it can prevent the headaches and cramps that come from sitting in a cold jail cell. A simple agreement with parents before the traveling season begins is strongly suggested. How simple? Well a statement to parents like the following is often all you need:

Dear Parent/Guardian:

During the season it may be necessary to contact you for unexpected transportation needs. For example, we may need to contact you if a bus arrives home early or late, if we have emergency transportation issues, or if your child needs to leave unexpectedly. For these reasons, please list your primary contact numbers (home and cell) plus three additional contacts that may be used if you cannot be reached. Should we not be able to reach any of the listed parties, please consider signing the consent statement to let us either arrange transportation or send your student home with another adult.

Please note that it is your responsibility to provide transportation to and from all school events in a timely and appropriate manner. This includes picking up and delivering students at announced times. Failure to provide transportation for your student may result in his or her exclusion from extracurricular and athletic participation.

If you have any questions about this request, please contact me as soon as possible.

Without the requested information, we will not be able to transport your student to school events.

Coach Hockets

It then becomes imperative that the coach follow up on collecting these forms and refusing to arrange transportation for any student who does not return the completed form. It is also much easier to enforce this process if it is included as a policy and/or procedure in the athletic handout or parent permission forms when the student first enrolls in an athletic or extracurricular activity. And it goes without saying, school districts should have their forms and policies reviewed by the school district's legal firm. They usually will do this for a nominal fee of $10,000. Just kidding about $10,000, but a few bucks spent ahead of time can prevent having to spend *mucho dinero* later.

And, of course, send a short note home before the first away game or event reminding parents of the policy and their obligation to provide transportation for their child.

There is one more thing to do ahead of time. All teachers who may, at some point, transport a student home or to the store or anywhere should be sure that they are covered under their auto insurance policy. I used to make certain that my coverage was significant for these types of situations, and while it cost me a few extra dollars to do so, it was well worth it.

But if we assume in this case study that the contact information process was not considered, Coach Hockets is now facing a situation with ninth-grade Amy, who is still crying. Amy tries calling her mom (a single parent) on her cell again—and still no answer. The nearest grandparent lives 600 miles away. She can't think of anyone else to call other than the next door neighbors—and she's not sure if her mom would want her riding with them. All the other kids have been picked up. Amy tells you that she told her mom to be at the school at 10:15 for the normal pickup.

The coach waits until 11:30 p.m. He calls the police to see if they are aware of any situations involving Amy's mom. Nothing. He decides to call the next door neighbor. She cannot leave her kids to come pick Amy up and her husband is out of town. No, she doesn't see any lights on next door but she is willing to go ring the bell. She calls back in a few minutes—no answer. The place seems empty.

Time for a Plan.

Coach Hocketts thinks about the situation. His principal, Karla B. Karefoil, has warned against driving students home. Randy has adequate insurance to drive students. Amy has asked if he would please take her home. He is worried about not only transporting her, but taking her to an empty house. He decides to call Principal Karefoil. The principal suggests he drive her home, but only after he does two things: (1) call the police to report the situation and meet him at the house and (2) post a large note on the school door indicating that Amy has been taken home. She also asks that he call her when he gets to the house. Coach Hockets adds one more task to the list—he calls his wife and gives her all the details of the trip, with Amy present.

In this case, every effort has been made to provide appropriate transportation and insure a safe situation at home.

Coach Hockets had no intention of leaving Amy outside by herself but was also very aware of the possible ramifications of simply driving her home or even letting her ride home with someone else. If another parent had agreed to take Amy home, without prior permission from Amy's mom, the coach should go through similar processes of notification before granting permission.

In this particular case, the police were present when Amy got home. She unlocked the door and the police stepped inside until Amy successfully located her mom, who had failed to adequately communicate with Amy about how she was getting home. The mother also had taken some cold medicine and fallen sound asleep—right through the calls and knocking. She subsequently suffered a bout of temporary, but severe embarrassment along with her cold.

Note again how a letter from Coach Hockets asking for three phone numbers to call and permission to arrange transportation for Amy would have entirely changed this situation. A little advanced planning can prevent the need for complicated and time-consuming last-minute solutions.

Chapter Two

Student Free Speech and Due Process Rights: Sex, Drugs, and Rock 'N' Roll

Brian D. Schwartz

Introduction

Perhaps the most challenging issues for teachers and administrators to effectively deal with is that of student constitutional rights. Today, a significant number of lawsuits that are filed against school districts, board members, administrators, teachers, and school employees involve a situation where a student has sought to assert his or her "constitutional rights."

In 1969 the United States Supreme Court addressed the issue of student constitutional rights in the now infamous case *Tinker v. Des Moines Independent Community School District*. In this case, John Tinker and two other students decided to wear black armbands to school in protest of the Vietnam War. School officials became aware of the plan and adopted a policy prohibiting this means of expression. Under the policy, a student who wore the armband would be asked to remove it. If the student refused, he or she would be suspended from school.

Tinker and his co-conspirators wore the armbands to school in violation of the policy and were subsequently suspended. In challenging the district's actions, the students asserted their First Amendment rights to free expression. The

United States Supreme Court found that "[i]t can hardly be argued that either students or teachers shed their constitutional rights to freedom of speech or expression at the schoolhouse gate." On the other hand, the Court recognized the special relationship between schools and students and the need to "prescribe and control conduct in the schools."

The Court ultimately ruled in favor of the student plaintiffs, finding that silent, passive expression, unaccompanied by any disorder, is akin to pure speech and is constitutionally protected under the First Amendment. Even in holding for Tinker, the Court announced its first exception to student speech, opining that any conduct that "would substantially interfere with the work of the school or impinge upon the rights of other students" could be prohibited by school officials.

In the nearly 40 years since the *Tinker* decision, the judicial system has heard a litany of constitutional challenges dealing with student speech, religion, due process, and right to be free from unreasonable search and seizure. This chapter seeks to discuss the current status of student First and Fourteenth Amendment constitutional rights and the rights of school officials to limit student constitutional protections under certain, limited circumstances. (We have decided to address First and Fourteenth Amendment issues together in this chapter due to the interplay of these student constitutional rights.) Chapter Three will examine the Fourth Amendment and student search and seizure issues.

Fourteenth Amendment: Student Due Process

Due process essentially gives students the right to tell their side of the story and defend their actions before being disciplined by school officials. However, the amount of due process generally depends on the severity of the deprivation or the significance of what is being taken away from the student.

Generally speaking, there are two types of due process to which students are entitled: substantive due process and procedural due process. While the distinction between the two is largely a matter for legal scholars to debate, procedural due process is essentially based on the concept of "fundamental fairness." As construed by the courts, this includes a student's right to be adequately apprised of rules and requirements to which the student will be held, to be adequately notified of charges and disciplinary proceedings, and the opportunity to be heard at these proceedings. Substantive due process, on the other hand, assures that rules and policies are clear and are not overtly unreasonable in nature.

For example, suppose that a group of students were engaged in a brutal fight at their high school's football game. Both students and members of the public were injured. Certainly, school officials would want to consider disciplining the students for their respective roles in the fight. From a substantive due process perspective, the policies under which the students are to be disciplined must be clear and inherently reasonable. A zero-tolerance policy, under which a certain conduct always results in a certain punishment despite mitigating circumstances, would very likely be a violation of substantive due process. Likewise, the students would need to be given an adequate opportunity to defend their actions. This is procedural due process.

As noted previously, the amount of procedural due process required largely depends on what is being taken away from the student. Most low-level punishments, such as a detention or withholding recess, do not require a teacher or administrator to provide a student with any due process whatsoever. Image the time and trouble it would take to provide a due process hearing to every student before being able to assign a detention!

However, greater levels of punishment that take away things of greater importance require enhanced due process protections. Again, the greater the depravation, the greater the due process that must be provided. Generally speaking, there are two student “punishments” that result in significant due process rights for students: suspension and expulsion.

According to the courts, a suspension is a short-term removal from school that can last up to ten school days. Because students facing temporary suspension from a public school have property and liberty interests in their education, they are entitled to a strict set of protection under the Due Process Clause of the Fourteenth Amendment. According to the United States Supreme Court in the case of *Goss v. Lopez*, a student must be given an oral or written notice of the charges against him and, if he denies them, an explanation of the evidence.

The student must also be given the opportunity to present his or her version of events to the suspending school official. Generally, the notice and opportunity to be heard should precede the student's removal from school, but if prior notice and an opportunity to be heard are not feasible, as where the student's presence endangers persons or property or threatens disruption of the academic process (thus justifying immediate removal from school), the necessary notice and opportunity to be heard should follow as soon as practicable.

Note that the above procedures are the minimum required by the federal courts to protect student rights. Each state or school district may, through law or policy, increase the due process protections given to students before being suspended from school.

The due process procedures required before a student is expelled are largely a matter of state law. However, it is clear that an expulsion is much more serious in nature than a suspension, so the amount of due process must be significantly more than what is required for suspensions under *Goss v. Lopez*. Most states require an opportunity for an extensive hearing before the school board before an expulsion goes into effect. Although these hearings are not trials, *per se*, many courts have afforded students trial-type rights, such as the right to be represented by an attorney, the right to present evidence, and a limited right to cross-examine witnesses. Again, school officials should consult the laws of their state and their school district policies when seeking to expel a student for gross misconduct.

Note also that the above scheme of due process does not apply to students who receive special education services. Students who receive special education services are generally entitled to enhanced due process rights under the Individuals with Disabilities Education Act and the corresponding laws of their respective state.

The other area of due process not yet discussed in detail involves the right of students to be free from unreasonably prescriptive policies or from being held to comply with policies that are so vague they cannot reasonably be interpreted. This is the substantive component to due process. In following notions of substantive due process, school officials must assure that their policies adequately put students on notice of the expectations to which they will be held. According to a majority of courts, school district policies need not be as detailed as criminal laws because the punishments schools are allowed to impose are significantly less severe than the punishments available under the criminal justice system. However, school district policies must generally be sufficient to put students on notice.

Substantive due process also requires school district policies and practices to be fundamentally fair. Although judges are remiss to put themselves in the shoes of school officials, it is clear that a policy or practice may not be so draconian or unfair that it "shocks the consciousness." Only when a school district policy or practice is so intolerably unjust that it violates every vestige of fundamental fairness is the policy or practice likely to be found unconstitutional by the courts.

First Amendment: Student Speech

When discussing student free speech rights, the first determination that must be made is whether or not a student's expression is considered to be speech. In order for student expression to be considered speech, the expression must (1) convey a particular message and (2) generally be capable of being understood by others.

For example, most student dress code matters are not First Amendment issues. A student does not have a constitutional right to wear shorts to school, wear a top that exposes the student's midriff, or wear "spaghetti-straps." These types of expression are not speech in that students do not convey a particular message by wearing these items of clothing. Furthermore, even if the student is attempting to convey a message in wearing these items of clothing, it is not a message that is readily capable of being understood by others.

Another example: Take the case of a male high school student who wore a baseball-style cap to school in violation of the school's "no hats" policy. The student, through his parents, sued the school district, claiming that his free speech rights were violated. The court first noted that the cap did not contain a message. When asked why he wore the hat, the student responded that he was trying to "look cool." The court found that the student's attire did not explicitly or implicitly convey a message and was therefore not speech, which might be entitled to constitutional protections.

In cases like those described above, where students are not engaging in speech, a school or school district can enact and enforce any rule or policy as long as the rule or policy is adequately publicized and has a reasonable educational purpose. Taking a second look at the above cases, there are a number of sound educational reasons for not allowing students to wear shorts, revealing clothing, or hats to school.

However, in cases where student expression or dress does convey a particular message and that message is generally understood by others, the student is engaging in speech. A student's speech is generally protected under the First Amendment. A school district can, however, limit a student's speech in cases where the speech is somehow exempt from First Amendment protections or the school district has an absolutely compelling reason to do so. The courts have recognized a limited number of situations where schools and districts are allowed to regulate or prohibit student speech. Speaking generally, the exceptions to free speech fit into the following categories:

- Speech that is substantially disruptive or materially interferes with school or district activities or the educational mission of the school or district;

- Alcohol and/or drug-related speech;
- Vulgar, lewd, obscene, or plainly offensive speech;
- Speech that is school-sponsored or part of the school's curriculum;
- Speech that causes a substantial health or safety concern, and
- Hate speech / true threats.

Still another example. Suppose that a student wears to school a t-shirt with big red letters reading "BUDWEISER." Again, the first question that must be asked is whether or not the student's t-shirt amounts to speech. In this case, the t-shirt clearly sends a message: "I like or support Budweiser beer." Here, the school or district can clearly prohibit the student from expressing this opinion and from wearing this t-shirt because it falls into one of the above-referenced exceptions to speech in that it promotes alcohol or drugs.

The above case is relatively simple, but illustrates the point. However, consider the following: A middle school student draws the image of a confederate flag on her notebook during class. Clearly, this image invokes some sort of message and should be considered speech. The next question that should be addressed is whether or not the school or district can prohibit the speech. In looking at the above exceptions to speech, there are several that may apply. However, without more information, we cannot really tell if the student's drawing is disruptive, hateful, or intends to convey a threat.

In situations like this, it is critical for teachers and administrators to carefully investigate the situation and document to see whether the t-shirt, drawing, or other expression in question falls into one or more of the exceptions to student speech. For a teacher or administrator to simply state that the expression is "disruptive," without more, is legally insufficient. It is critical to show *how* the expression is disruptive. In the case of the drawing of the confederate flag, this can be done by showing a past history of race-related incidents at the school or by documenting that several students indicated that they felt threatened or uncomfortable with the image.

In reexamining the BUDWEISER t-shirt example, documentation is not necessary because the exact wording of the t-shirt is the actual violation. However, in a vast majority of cases, the exception to student speech is not clear on its face. Documentation, documentation, and more documentation is the key in being able to substantiate your actions!

At the risk of belaboring the point, let me call your attention to one more example. Shortly after the United States Supreme Court upheld the right of the *Tinker* plaintiffs to wear their black armbands in protest of the Vietnam War, a similar case surfaced. In *Guzick v. Drebus*, students sought to wear buttons promoting an anti-war demonstration in Chicago. When the school punished the students for wearing the buttons at school, legal scholars predicted an outcome similar to the one in *Tinker*: that the buttons amounted to pure, non-disruptive speech and were therefore allowable. However, in this case, the federal appellate court found in favor of the school district. Here, the school administration was able to successfully document that these buttons advertised a racist ant-war protest and that several African-American students had expressed apprehension and concern over the buttons. Hence, a material and substantial disruption—or at least a substantial likelihood of one—was shown to exist.

Another exception to student speech that is frequently debated centers around what constitutes "obscene" language or conduct. Here, it is again important to remember that the free speech rights of students are not automatically co-extensive with the rights of adults in other settings. However, courts do not like overly sensitive teachers or administrators who are offended by every vintage of student speech or expression. As a general rule, the age of the students, community standards, and general common sense should help guide what conduct is acceptable and what conduct is obscene or otherwise inappropriate.

In 1986, the United States Supreme Court specifically addressed the subject of lewd and obscene speech in the case of *Bethel School District No. 403 v. Frazier*. Here, a high school senior gave a speech nominating a fellow student for student council vice president. The speech was filled with sexual innuendos, prompting discipline from school officials. In a 7 to 2 decision, the Court upheld the discipline of the student, finding that "[f]reedom to advocate unpopular and controversial views in schools and classrooms must be balanced against society's countervailing interest in teaching students boundaries of socially appropriate behavior." More specifically, the Court held: "First Amendment jurisprudence recognizes interest in protecting minors from exposure to vulgar and offensive spoken language, as well as limitations on otherwise absolute interest of speaker in reaching unlimited audience where speech is sexually explicit and audience may include children."

Schools and districts can also put restrictions on speech that is part of the school's curriculum or speech that is school-sponsored. Take for example the United States Supreme Court case of *Hazelwood v. Kuhlmeier*. Here, a student asserted First Amendment protections in attempting to publish articles about pregnancy and divorce in the school newspaper. The high Court ruled that curricular school newspapers and other school-sponsored publications are subject to a lower level of First Amendment protection and that schools can impose reasonable, viewpoint-neutral editorial control. The school's decision that the articles on pregnancy and divorce were not appropriate was therefore proper.

Schools and districts also have wide latitude in prohibiting speech or conduct that is a health or safety concern. For example, a school or district may prohibit students from wearing jewelry that may cause injury during physical education class or while participating in athletic activities. It is important to note that these types of limitations on student speech are extremely temporary in nature. In this example, students are free to resume their free expression after the conclusion of the event.

Rounding out the list of speech that can be regulated is that of hate speech and true threats. A school district's ability to curtail hate speech is still mostly undecided. In 1942, in *Chaplinsky v. New Hampshire*, the United States Supreme Court found that government entities (including school districts) can prohibit "fighting words," as they serve no legitimate redeeming value and can incite violent retaliation. In recent years, the fighting words / hate speech doctrine has developed into a debate between "words" and "actions." A school policy prohibiting words alone is constitutionally suspect, whereas a policy prohibiting hateful words that are likely to constitute a true threat is more likely to be upheld.

First Amendment: Freedom of Religion

Perhaps no right is more revered that an individual's freedom of religion and religious expression. In the above discussion on student speech, we saw several areas where the courts are willing to limit the extent of free speech and expression. When it comes to religious rights, however, the courts have been more hesitant to allow school districts to impose restrictions on students.

Any school rule or district policy that burdens a student's freedom of religion is examined with the strictest scrutiny. In a nutshell, such rules or policies must be absolutely necessary to meet a legitimate educational goal or interest, must be narrowly tailored, and must be the least restrictive means available for meeting the legitimate purpose. As is evident, this extremely restrictive test makes a school district's intrusion into the area of student religious freedom very daunting.

Generally, the above test has allowed school districts to impose some time and place restrictions on students' free exercise of religion; however, restrictions on the manner in which a student may pray are strictly prohibited. For example, a school district, for obvious pedagogical reasons, can prohibit a student from engaging in prayer during instructional time. When not engaged in school activities or instruction, students are free to pray and conduct other religious exercises, subject to the school's rules designed to prevent material disruption of the educational program.

In accordance with guidance issued by the United States Department of Education, freedom of religion includes "the right of students to read their Bibles or other scriptures, say grace before meals, and pray or study religious materials with fellow students during recess, the lunch hour, or other non-instructional time to the same extent that they may engage in nonreligious activities. While school authorities may impose rules of order and pedagogical restrictions on student activities, they may not discriminate against student prayer or religious speech in applying such rules and restrictions."

Additionally, students may organize prayer groups, religious clubs, and "see you at the pole" gatherings before and after school. Such groups must be given the same access to school facilities as is given to other non school-related student organizations.

Perhaps the one area that has been subject to the greatest debate is the right of students to pray at school events, such as an athletic contest or graduation. There have been a number of court cases that have balanced the rights of students to engage in such practices with the constitutional requirements mandating a separation of church and state. As a general rule of thumb, students can pray or lead a prayer at a school event as long as the prayer is purely student initiated. For example, the captain of the football team could lead the team in a prayer before the big game, as long as the prayer was completely student initiated and student led. It would be a violation of the Establishment Clause of the First Amendment for the team's coach to either select a student to lead a prayer or suggest that students engage in prayer. It would also be impermissible for the coach to pray with the students; however, the coach may be present during the prayer as long as his presence is strictly supervisory in nature.

Like religious speech, students have considerable rights in terms of religious dress. Again, it is important to emphasize that students can wear religious garb unless the school or district can show an absolutely compelling reason to curtail this expression. A review of applicable case law suggests that schools and districts should make every opportunity to accommodate aspects of student religious dress. This includes the right of Jewish and Muslim students to wear traditional religious headgear despite the school district's "no hats" policy. Also included would be the right of Hindu students to wear traditional regalia despite a school district's safety policies prohibiting similar types of dress among the general student population.

Conclusion

Based on the above discussion, it is clear that students have constitutional rights while at school. It is equally clear that these rights are not the same rights as the ones enjoyed by adults in other settings. The constitutional rights most challenged by students involve First Amendment freedom of speech and religion and Fourteenth Amendment due process protections.

When dealing with student constitutional rights, it is extremely important to know the current state of the law, as failure to do so can result in not only liability against the school district, but also personal liability against the school official handling the situation. In summary, it is important to remember the following information.

First Amendment Freedom of Speech: The first question that must be asked is whether or not the student's expression constitutes speech. Speech generally involves a student intending to send a particular message and that message being generally understood by others. If the expression is not speech, school officials may adopt rules, regulations, and policies that have a reasonable educational purpose. If the student's expression does constitute speech, the student's conduct may only be barred if it falls into certain delineated exceptions to speech. Careful and complete documentation by school officials is critical when it comes to enforcing restrictions on student freedom of speech.

First Amendment Freedom of Religion: Students enjoy heightened constitutional rights when it comes to freedom of religion. School officials can usually impose reasonable time and place restrictions, but can never interfere with the manner in which students practice their religion. Time and place restrictions are generally limited to instructional time. Additionally, school officials should consult with their attorney any time that student dress is at issue.

Fourteenth Amendment Due Process: Students are entitled to due process, or an opportunity to tell their side of the story and defend their actions. The amount of due process generally depends on the deprivation involved. The less serious the punishment, like a detention, the lesser amount of due process that is required. The more serious the punishment, such as a suspension or expulsion, the greater the opportunity for a student to defend himself or herself. Also implicit in the scheme of due process is a right of students to be notified in advance of the rules, regulations, and expectations to which they will be held. School officials are also prohibited from adopting policies or otherwise engaging in practices that are inherently unreasonable.

Case Study #2: Tommy and Marilyn—Not What you Think!

Tommy Troublemaker is a sixth grade student at Freedom Middle School. After attending a "Marilyn Manson" concert on the previous night, Tommy proudly wore his concert t-shirt to school. The t-shirt depicts gothic symbols and contains an image of Marilyn Manson that some students may find frightening. The t-shirt does not contain any language, other than listing the concert tour dates. Seeing the t-shirt after lunch, the Principal instructs Tommy that the t-shirt is inappropriate and directs Tommy to either change clothes or turn the t-shirt inside out. Tommy refuses and is disciplined.

Legal Perspective:

Some version of these facts has played itself out in practically every school in America. A student seeks to express himself or herself and school authorities find the student's expression somehow inappropriate. Situations involving student expression must be analyzed in accordance with the two-step test discussed earlier in this chapter. The first question that must be asked is whether or not the student's expression constitutes speech.

In order to be considered speech, the student must be expressing a particular message that must generally be understood by others. If the student's expression is not speech, school officials may impose any policies or rules that are educationally reasonable. If the student's expression does constitute speech, school officials may only limit the speech if it falls into one of the enumerated exceptions to speech, as authorized by the courts.

In this case, the student's t-shirt constitutes speech. The student is clearly expressing a message and anyone seeing the student clearly understands what that message is: "I am a fan of Marilyn Manson." Hence, in order to discipline the student for wearing the t-shirt to school, school officials must be able to show that one or more of the exceptions to speech applies. Here, one plausible exception to speech is that the student's t-shirt is substantially disruptive or materially interferes with school activities or the educational mission of the school.

Case closed, correct? Not so fast. A teacher or administrator's unilateral determination that a t-shirt is substantially disruptive or a material interference, by itself, is legally insufficient. This is not the case of the BUDWEISER t-shirt, as discussed above, where the message on the shirt is the actual exception to speech in that it expresses a reference to alcohol. Here, the t-shirt may or may not be disruptive depending on the circumstances. It is therefore critical for the principal to document exactly *how* the t-shirt is disruptive. This evidence must come from teachers, students, and others who are directly negatively impacted by the t-shirt in question.

You will note from the facts in this case that the principal did not become aware of the student's t-shirt until he saw the student wearing it after lunch. We must assume from these facts that no one was concerned about the t-shirt to the extent that it was brought to the attention of the principal throughout the entire morning. It may therefore appear that the t-shirt is not overtly disruptive and the principal is reacting based entirely on his subjective judgment.

In light of the above facts, the principal may wish to take a different approach in seeking to prohibit the student from wearing this particular t-shirt. You will remember that another exception to free speech occurs when the speech is vulgar, lewd, obscene, or plainly offensive. Here, as a general rule, the age of the students, community standards, and general common sense should be taken into account in determining if the t-shirt is appropriate.

In looking at the facts from our case study once again, it should be noted that this incident has taken place at a middle school. The standard of what is appropriate and what is not appropriate with this age range of students is often the most difficult. Even more difficult in this case is the fact that the t-shirt does not explicitly contain any clearly offensive language or inappropriate symbols; rather, some student simply might be frightened by the picture on the t-shirt. As there has not been a significant reaction to the t-shirt throughout the morning—as is evidenced by the fact that the matter was not brought to the principal's attention earlier—the principal's actions in disciplining the student for refusing to remove the t-shirt probably run afoul of the Constitution and thus violate the student's freedom of speech.

As the above scenario shows, teachers and administrators must be very careful in curtailing student constitutional rights. Careful documentation based on the accounts of students and teachers is often key in proving an exception to student speech. However—and I hate the expression—there is more than one way to skin a cat. Despite the legal restrictions placed on the principal in this scenario, there may be other ways to deal with this and similar situations that encourage students not to engage in forms of expression that bend, but do not break, the rules. Jim will now explore these and other related issues.

Administrative Perspective:

Before I begin, I must admit that I'm a seasoned administrator. You know, I am a veteran, experienced, er, old. When I think of Marilyn, I don't think of Manson. When I think of Marilyn, it is Monroe, and if not Monroe, it is at least a female. Now I said I was old, but not completely out-of-touch. I know who Marilyn Manson is, and once, by accident, I listened to him sing. And, I'll admit it, I don't get it—the dress, the dancing, the music, the persona. But then I guess kids today would think naming a group the Four Tops is as strange as I think the name Nine Inch Nails. So be it, generation gaps, changes in culture, different strokes for different—never mind, you get it, but I guess the principal doesn't. Without any input or any guidance, he disciplines Tommy for wearing a shirt featuring someone Tommy apparently likes—who may have contributed to Tommy's need for hearing aids before he hits 45. It makes me wonder if any kids were ever disciplined for wearing Tiny Tim t-shirts? He sure scared the beegeebees out of me!

At first blush I would say this case is no case. Barry is the one who has over-reacted by disciplining Tommy. Barry finds the t-shirt to be potentially frightening to other students, and yet no one has complained. And I have to wonder what middle school student would be frightened by a Marilyn Manson t-shirt anyway. We are told the t-shirt is not vulgar nor does it sport anything promoting drugs or sex or other inappropriate topics. It may be offensive only if you don't like hard rock performed by a guy with girl's name and lots of make-up.

I'm a Cubs fan and I know that near St. Louis my Cubs shirts are highly offensive to those with questionable baseball taste, but that is still no reason to punish me for being brighter than everyone else.

I'm willing to back up a minute and give Barry some space. Maybe there is some history I don't know about, or maybe he truly feels the shirt could cause someone to shake in their Nikes, or maybe he feels that middle school kids and/or teachers could be distracted from learning by peeking at the lovely Marilyn. If he did feel this way, wouldn't Barry do his homework before tempting fate with his punishment? At the very least, shouldn't he have checked to see if the shirt fit the policy for distracting or inappropriate clothing? Or maybe he should ask another administrator for his opinion, or even utilze the attorney retainer provision and called the lawyer for a quick consult.

An alternative to jumping the gun might be, in addition to checking the policy and getting a second opinion, talking to one of Tommy's teachers that day to see if the teacher remembered, or even noticed, the t-shirt, and if so, whether it caused a distraction. If the answer is "no," then maybe a heart-to-heart with Tommy about why Barry doesn't like the t-shirt might be appropriate, with a request not to wear the shirt again, please. However, my first guess would be that if no one else is bothered, drop it. Aren't there better things to do like evaluate the teacher down the hall that has marginal discipline?

It's quite possible that nothing will happen to Barry even though he was probably out of line by his disciplinary dictates because Tommy's parents may not really like Marilyn all that well themselves. On the other hand, it's quite possible that the parents will become madder than a hornet. If they do, it could be Barry who gets stung.

Bottom line is this. Pick your battles; know your options; do what is best for kids. Last night I watched a music awards show on TV. The performers ranged from a talking/singing Neil Diamond to Lil' YoMan, or something like that. Their dress ranged from falling-off pants to tuxedos. Paul McCartney did an old Beatles song and Justin Timberlake did a duet with a rapper—one guy was jumping all over the stage while the other one was crooning slow and easy. It was kind of fun. My point? We have to realize the difference in generations, taste, and style. It's not all bad, nor is it all inappropriate. Tommy, you win this one. Barry, do your homework. Marilyn, I still won't be buying your albums. And Neil, it's time to retire.

Chapter Three

Search and Seizure: Stripping Away the Misconceptions

Brian D. Schwartz

Introduction

Throughout much of history, it was unclear whether or not there were any parameters on schools and school personnel regarding searching students and students' possessions. Many legal scholars of the time opined that school officials, who stand *in loco parentis*, may search students and their possessions with or without suspicion. The legal reasoning behind this argument was as follows: Parents do not need any reason to conduct a search of their child, so neither do school officials who stand in place of the parent while the child is at school.

In 1985, the United States Supreme Court set the record straight and clearly defined the role and authority of school officials to conduct student searches. The case, *New Jersey v. T.L.O.*, involved a high school age female student who was suspected of smoking cigarettes in a school bathroom. T.L.O. claimed that she had never smoked cigarettes in her life, so she was taken to the assistant principal for further investigation. The assistant principal confiscated T.L.O.'s purse and opened it, finding cigarettes. When the assistant principal removed the cigarettes, he also saw rolling papers, which he believed were indicative of drug use. Upon further inspection of the purse, the assistant principal found a small amount of marijuana, a pipe, a large amount of money and an index card that appeared to contain the names of people who owed T.L.O. money. T.L.O. was taken to the police station where she was charged with delinquency.

T.L.O., through her parents, challenged the authority of school authorities to search her purse, claiming that their actions violated her Fourth Amendment right to be free from unreasonable search and seizure. Critical to her argument was the fact that school officials did not possess a warrant prior to initiating the search of her purse.

In resolving T.L.O.'s claim, the high Court recognized the fact that the Fourth Amendment does not forbid all searches; it only prohibits "unreasonable" searches. The Court went on to recognize that while students retain their constitutional rights while at school, these rights are not the same rights enjoyed by adults in other settings.

In a 6-3 decision, the Court held that school officials are not required to have probable cause or a warrant before searching students, but that school officials must possess "reasonable suspicion" before engaging in searches of students and student property. Furthermore, the Court held that school officials must have reasonable suspicion at the inception of the search and reasonable suspicion to expand the search beyond its original scope.

In the *T.L.O.* case, the Court ruled that the assistant principal had reasonable suspicion to search the student's purse. Specifically, there was strong evidence that the student had been smoking and it was reasonable to believe that evidence of smoking—the cigarettes—could be found in her purse. The Court also ruled that the expanded search of the student's purse for drug contraband was also reasonable in scope. When the assistant principal pulled the cigarettes out of the student's purse, the rolling papers were in plain view. Given the assistant principal's experience and expertise, it was reasonable for him to believe that the rolling papers were indicative of drug use and that further evidence of such drug use might be found in the student's purse. Hence, the search was reasonable at its inception and reasonable in scope.

Since 1985, the courts have heard a myriad of student search and seizure cases; however, all cases go back to the core pronouncements of *T.L.O.* Searches of students and their possessions must be reasonable at their inception and reasonable in scope. No matter what the issue, no matter what the subject of the search, these are the questions that must be addressed.

In determining whether a search is reasonable at its inception, courts have looked at a litany of factors. An examination of case law suggests that the primary factors that courts weigh in determining whether school officials are justified in initiating a search are (1) the nature of the infraction, (2) the invasiveness of the place to be searched, (3) the quality and quantity of informant information, and (4) individualized suspicion. I like to call these the "Four 'I's of Inception": **I**nfraction, **I**nvasiveness, **I**nformant information and **I**ndividualized suspicion.

In examining the above indicators, the most important factor is the nature of the infraction or, more specifically, what school officials are looking for. Courts are willing to grant school officials considerably more latitude and require considerably less evidence if the search is for a weapon or drugs. A good rule of thumb appears to be that the more dangerous the subject of the search, the less evidence that is needed. The less dangerous the subject of the search, the more evidence that is needed. However, it is important to recognize that some evidence will always be needed before a search can be initiated. Searches based on a hunch or mere speculation will generally be deemed unreasonable and therefore a violation of the Fourth Amendment.

In looking at the second factor—the invasiveness of the place to be searched—courts generally require more evidence the closer the search is to the student. For example, in order for a search to be reasonable, a school official would need more evidence to search a student directly and less evidence before searching a student's backpack or purse. For this reason, it is again a good rule of thumb to begin the search as far away from the student as possible and gradually move toward the student. In terms of a practical example, we can again turn to the *T.L.O.* case. Here, the assistant principal first searched the student's purse rather than initiating a more obtrusive search of the student directly.

Good informant information is also a key factor in determining whether or not reasonable suspicion exists to initiate a search. Because school officials generally do not see the infraction take place directly, they must investigate the situation and rely on the observations of others. In doing a thorough investigation, a school official must determine the credibility of the individuals supplying the information. The less credible the source, the more information that must be gathered before conducting a search.

Lastly, courts also want to see some degree of individualized suspicion before school officials initiate a search. Take, for example, a typical school classroom. Suppose that as the teacher turns her back to write on the board, her cell phone goes missing. It would be improper and a violation of the Fourth Amendment for the teacher to search all of the students in the classroom. The teacher would be required to investigate and obtain information from the students in order to significantly narrow the list of suspects. When the investigation points to one or two students, a search may be justified.

In order to bring the above factors into perspective, consider the following situation. During a passing period at Typical High School, a teacher overhears an unknown student indicate that Alex Jones has marijuana in his pocket. The teacher brings the situation to the attention of the principal, who must now investigate. Here, we have a fairly significant infraction (marijuana), but no immediate safety threat, an invasive place to be searched (Alex directly), individual suspicion, but bad informant information (an unknown student).

Based on these facts, there probably is not reasonable suspicion to immediately proceed with searching Alex's pockets for evidence of the suspected infraction. The principal must investigate to obtain better information. This may involve talking to Alex's friends or even talking to Alex himself. Once the principal has better evidence and has reasonable suspicion that Alex possesses the contraband in question, the principal should start the search in the least obtrusive place that the marijuana could reasonably be found. Under this approach, the search may start at the locker, proceed to a book bag, and finally end up with a search of Alex himself.

Now suppose that the unidentified student indicated that Alex has a gun. Assume that all other facts in the above scenario are the same. In this case, despite the weak informant information and the invasiveness of the place to be searched, the nature of the infraction (an immediate threat to student safety) would generally justify an immediate search of Alex without the need for additional evidence. The search would be reasonable given the overriding need for school officials to protect life and property.

One last point is important to note. If the student who is the subject of the investigation authorizes you to conduct a search, then you may do so without additional evidence. Authorization by the person subject to the search takes the search out of the context of the Fourth Amendment, with the possible exception of automobile searches, which will be discussed later in this chapter. Hence, it is always a good practice to talk to the student in question in order to attempt to secure permission to conduct a search. Doing so may save a great deal of time and effort otherwise required in order to obtain reasonable suspicion.

So far, we have discussed the factors that determine whether or not school officials can initiate a search of a student or student property. The second prong of the test delineated in *T.L.O.* requires that a search be reasonable in scope. Again, courts take several factors into consideration in determining the depth in which a search can proceed. However, an analysis of case law suggests that the two most important factors are (1) the search objective and (2) the seriousness of the allegation. I like to call these two factors the "Two 'S's of Scope": **S**earch objective and **S**eriousness of the allegation.

The search objective, put simply, means that school officials must only search in those places where it is reasonable to believe that the object of the search can be located. For example, if school officials are searching for a five-inch knife, it would be unreasonable to search in a small zippered compartment of a purse where a five-inch knife would not reasonably fit.

The second criteria, the seriousness of the allegation, means that the search should not be excessive given the item being sought and should not be inappropriate given the age and sex of the student. Again, in terms of an example, it would be inherently unreasonable to conduct a strip search of a student to look for a stolen five-dollar bill. Here, the means for recovering the stolen property are abhorrently excessive given the nature of the suspected activity. In terms of the age and sex of the child, special considerations should be made to protect the child's dignity and privacy. In cases where a strip search may be reasonable, it is important to make sure the search is done by someone of the same sex as the child as well as to provide the child with alternative clothing so as not to unnecessarily embarrass the child.

With this basic framework in place, let's take a look at specific types of searches. In particular, we will examine locker searches, vehicle searches, metal detector searches, dog-aided searches, police-assisted searches, and random drug testing.

Specific Types of Student Searches

Locker Searches: It is important for school officials to consult their state's law and school district policy before engaging in a locker search. In general, locker searches are generally among the least invasive types of searches. Students have a diminished expectation of privacy in their lockers, mainly because lockers are school property.

Vehicle Searches: Vehicle searches are somewhat tricky due to the fact that the vehicle may be owned by a party other than the student. Vehicles owned by a student's parents may generally only be searched by police pursuant to a warrant. Again, state law governs vehicle searches. However, one common practice is for school officials to require a copy of a vehicle's registration and a written consent to search from the student and the vehicle's owner before a student is allowed to park on school property.

Metal Detectors: Metal detector searches are minimally invasive in that a machine or device screens the person who passes through it. Individuals subject to the search are not required to remove items of clothes or be searched directly by a person. Given the heightened need for school safety, metal detector searches are generally legal as long as they are done in a completely random manner or everyone, including school employees and visitors, are required to undergo the search before entering the school building.

Dog Searches: Dog searches are generally legal, as long as the dog is in the public areas of the school. A dog's heightened sense of smell, special training, and lack of bias make dog searches inherently reasonable. However, dogs should not be used to search students directly, as this type of search may be unreasonable in scope and may therefore violate the Fourth Amendment.

Police-Aided Searches: In general, police officers may assist school officials in conducting a search, as long as officers are acting under the direction of school authorities. When police officers act on their own initiative, probable cause supported by a warrant is generally required. One exception may exist for police liaison officers who, in certain states, are considered school officials and are therefore allowed to conduct searches with only reasonable suspicion.

Random Drug Testing: The ability of school districts to impose random drug testing was addressed by the United States Supreme Court in 1995 in *Vernonia School District 47J v. Acton*. In this case, the school district instituted a system of random, suspicionless drug testing of student athletes. The

Court held that the school district's policy was reasonable based on the following factors: a drug culture that was prominent among student athletes, privacy considerations that were in place, the fact that the results of positive tests were not used for academic penalties, the fairness of the drug testing selection process, and other factors. It is important to note that *Vernonia* only applies to random drug testing of student athletes. In 2002, in *Board of Education v. Earls*, the U.S. Supreme Court (by a 5 to 4 vote) extended random, suspicionless drug tests to students engaged in all extracurricular activities.

Seizure of Students

To this point we have only discussed student searches. The Fourth Amendment also requires reasonableness when a student is seized or restrained. A seizure under the Fourth Amendment occurs any time a student's movement is restricted either by physical force or exercise of authority. This would include a school official standing in front of a door and refusing to let a student leave or threatening a student with disciplinary consequences if the student leaves the room. If a student is free to walk away, the Fourth Amendment is not implicated.

In determining if a student seizure is reasonable, courts generally look at the "circumstances then existing and apparent," or the nature and urgency of the circumstances at the time that school officials needed to seize a student. Courts also generally consider the same types of factors as they do with student searches. The more compelling the reason that school officials have for detaining a student, the more likely that the seizure will be deemed reasonable. For example, the detention of a student suspected of having a weapon or drugs will be allowed with significantly less evidence than would ordinarily be required if the student were suspected of possessing a stolen library book.

When it comes to seizing or restraining a student for safety reasons, a short-term seizure is generally reasonable if the school official who is restraining the student does not use excessive force and releases the student as soon as it is safe to do so. However, sometimes it is necessary for school officials to restrain students for an extended period of time in order to assure the safety of that student and others. In these cases, many states require school officials to have specialized training. This specialized training then makes the long-term restraint reasonable.

Consequences for Improper Searches and Seizures

At this point, the reader may ask why conducting an appropriate search or seizure is so important. The answer is that evidence obtained pursuant to an improperly conducted search or seizure cannot generally be used to discipline a student. Furthermore, law enforcement personnel may also have their hands tied when attempting to follow up on criminal activity in cases where the underlying search or seizure by school officials was not conducted properly. Also important to note is the fact that lawsuits involving violations of student constitutional rights are brought in federal court, where there are fewer immunities and defenses available to school defendants and monetary judgments tend to be higher than in state court.

Conclusion

Whenever school officials undertake a search of a student or a student's possessions or attempt to restrain a student's movement (seizure), they must have reasonable suspicion to do so. The courts have generally given school officials considerable latitude to conduct searches or detain students in situations where there is an imminent threat to health or safety. The courts have also made it clear, however, that searches and seizures cannot take place based on a hunch or mere speculation. It is critically important that school officials conduct school searches and seizures in a "reasonable" manner in order to protect themselves and others and to preserve evidence.

In conducting searches, a good reference is the "Four 'I's of Inception" (**I**nfraction, **I**ntrusiveness, **I**nformant information, and **I**ndividualized suspicion) and the "Two 'S's of Scope" (**S**earch objective and **S**eriousness of the allegation).

Case Study #3:
Matt Mischief and the Blundered Search

Lynne is a freshman student at Miranda High School, which is a large suburban public high school located in Anytown, USA. While riding the bus to school one morning, Lynne overhears another student, Matt Mischief, talk about his new switchblade knife, which Matt claims to have in his backpack. Matt does not show anyone the knife, nor does he make any threats. Although Lynne doubts that Matt actually has the knife because he is a "big talker," she decides to bring the matter to the attention of the school principal. The principal, knowing that there is a school policy against bringing knives to school, immediately finds Matt and without saying a word, grabs and searches his backpack. No knife is found. The principal then takes Matt to his office and proceeds to search Matt by requiring him to remove all of his clothes. Matt, who is now stripped down to his underwear, is cold and terribly embarrassed. Still, no knife is found. The principal allows Matt to get dressed and proceed to class.

Legal Perspective:

This case study certainly gives us a lot of material with which to work! Before we look at the facts, however, I think it is important to make two general observations. First, I want to point out a bit of a red herring in the above scenario. The fact that no knife is ever found is irrelevant to the situation. What is important is that the search itself is conducted properly. If a proper search is conducted, the fact that the contraband in question is not located does not invalidate the search or increase the liability of the party who conducted the search.

Second, it is important to remember that the Fourth Amendment is only implicated if the student in question does not consent to the search. If the student allows the school official to search or agrees to empty out his or her pockets, the student has forgone Fourth Amendment protections. Hence, it is critical for a school official to first ask the student to consent to the search. If consent is obtained, Fourth Amendment concerns are mitigated.

Okay, now on to the facts of this specific case study.

As we discussed above, searches of students at school must be reasonable at their inception and reasonable in scope. Both of these elements are required in order for a search to withstand Fourth Amendment scrutiny. In terms of being reasonable at its inception, it is important to determine if the principal has enough information or evidence to search Matt's backpack. Here, it is important to remember the four "I"s of inception. Again, these are the primary factors that a court will look at to determine if the search was properly initiated and include the following: (1) the nature of the infraction, (2) the intrusiveness of the place to be searched, (3) the quality and quantity of informant information, and (4) individualized suspicion.

In this case, the nature of the infraction is quite serious: we have a student potentially with a knife at school. Likewise, we have individual suspicion: there is only one suspect. In terms of informant information, it is important for the principal to access and document the credibility of Lynne. Due to the seriousness of the infraction, the search can probably proceed if Lynne is at all credible. In other words, given the seriousness of a knife potentially being at school, there probably is not time to conduct a full-scale investigation, including interviewing other students. However, had Matt been bragging about having a stolen library book, it would be advisable to get additional information before conducting the search.

In turning our attention to the scope of the search, it is again important to remember the two "S's" of scope: (1) the search objective, and (2) the seriousness of the allegation. With respect to the search objective, we need to assure that the object of the search (the knife) could reasonably be found in the places that are being searched. Here again, it is reasonable to believe that a knife could be in the student's backpack. However, it may or may not be reasonable to believe that the student could hide the knife on his person in areas that would require him to remove almost all items of clothing.

Where this search probably fails, however, is in the second prong of the scope test, or the seriousness of the allegation. Although a knife is certainly a serious matter, the manner in which the student was strip-searched was most likely excessive. I am not suggesting that a well-executed strip search would be deemed unreasonable. However, the manner in which the principal executed this particular strip search appears, on its face, to be clearly excessive. The principal could probably have let the student keep a majority of his clothing in tact during the search. At the very least, the student should have been given an article of clothing to put on for every article of clothing he was asked to remove.

Lastly, it is worth mentioning that the principal should, for his own protection, have had another person in the room at the time the search was being conducted. Additionally, both the principal and the observer should be the same sex as the student being searched to further assure student privacy.

I now turn to Jim, who will certainly have some good advice regarding the practicality of how the search was handled by the principal.

Administrative Perspective:

As a school administrator one of my primary jobs is to protect the safety of everyone: students, staff, visitors, stray dogs, and even myself. Can they be too safe? That's a hard one to answer, but we all agree, especially in this day and age, that safety is paramount in the operation of any public activity or gathering. So when Lynne comes to my office and, with some reluctance, offers the suggestion that Matt has a knife, my focus becomes directed toward safety. Everything else is on hold.

Let's go three ways with Lynne's report. Let's first assume we know Lynne, trust her judgment, and have no qualms about her report. That was easy. On the other hand, let's assume we don't know Lynne, don't know her relationship to Matt, don't know if she is sure about what she heard, and we aren't convinced that her story is reliable. We just aren't sure. And finally, let's assume we know Lynne has some issues. She has been in trouble and a lot of her problems revolved around her various interpretations of the truth. And, we remember a verbal fight that Lynne and Matt were in recently. We think they dated once and now are no longer friends. So the question is this: what do we do based on which of the Lynnes we are talking to?

For me, there is no choice—because of the knife. Lynne #1 makes it easy. Find Matt; locate and remove the knife. Lynne #2 makes me think a little more on the way to find Matt and locate/remove the knife. Lynne #3 will really make me mad if I can't find the knife when I find Matt. Do you hear what I am saying? You have been told a kid has a knife. You have no choice but to find Matt, then try to find the knife.

What Brian says about the quality and quantity of information when it comes to a weapon or a bomb or an attempt to kill or injure doesn't really matter in my mind. Even if Lynne were stark raving mad, foaming at the mouth, and spinning six hula hoops while she reported that Matt had a knife, I would still go and find Matt to see if a knife exists. You can't take threats or situations like this lightly. This is probably why I cancelled school fairly quickly when ice or snow or dangerous roads were forecast. My heart and my head always agreed that it was pretty hard to slide a bus into a ditch or into the lane of another vehicle in May, but why take the chance in January?

So far I agree with the principal in his assessment that Matt needs to be located and a search for the knife needs to begin. However, we differ from this point on. The principal seems to have a little Inspector Clouseau in him. I like to think I have watched enough *Law and Order*, and attended enough sessions with Brian, to know that the accused have rights and that I am subject to great scrutiny if I screw up the investigation. So, step one, find another male administrator or teacher to go with me as I search for Matt.

Let's assume Matt is in class. So as not to draw undo attention or cause a stir, I ask my counterpart to stand in the doorway as I enter the room and quietly call the teacher aside and tell her I need to talk to Matt for a moment. I then walk over to Matt and tell him I need to talk with him briefly in the hall. I walk with Matt to the hall, and then the three of us find an area that is private and yet close to the hall to talk. One needs to prepare for the worse case options while still being fair and prudent. My first comment would be that it has come to our attention that Matt announced he had brought a knife to school and we would like to take possession of it. At that point I would ask for his cooperation in telling us where the knife is. When he says he does not have a knife, I would then ask for his backpack and tell him I am going to search for the knife. I would do so with Matt and the teacher present. I would then ask the teacher to search the backpack if I could not find the knife, just to make sure I didn't somehow miss it.

Next I would ask Matt if he has a weapon on his person. When he says he does not, I would then inform him I need to search him to make sure there is no weapon on his body. I would ask him once more if he has the weapon and if he understands what we are doing and why.

First, in the privacy of an office, I would ask Matt to remove his shirt and empty all his pockets. I would then return his shirt and ask him to remove his shoes. Finally I would ask him to remove his pants. Unless he was wearing unusually bulky underwear that could conceal a knife taped to his leg or thigh, I would give him his pants back. If there was any chance that Matt might have a knife concealed under his underwear, I would inform him I was going to call the police and have them continue the search unless he wanted to remove his underwear quickly. As I mentioned, it would probably not be necessary to go this far with the search, but if my partner and I both felt it was necessary, we would do it.

Finally, we would walk Matt to his main locker and his gym locker. We would also contact his teachers to see if Matt has any storage areas (art cabinet, shop locker, football duffle bag), and we would proceed with a search of these areas as well. If Matt has a car, I would probably call our attorney for guidance with the search of the vehicle, after checking the school policy as it relates to cars on campus.

If, after all of this, including the responses from Matt, we feel he does not have a knife, we then begin the discussion of why he said he did. Matt can go two ways here: he can deny saying it or give us a reason. If he denies saying anything about a knife, I would hold him in a secure room and interview Lynne again. If I am sure he said it, then it is my turn to play inspector and get down to the truth. When I finally get Matt to admit he was being stupid when he joked about the knife, that is when we have a phone call to the parents about the entire situation and determine what discipline will be appropriate for the action.

Brian's test of the 4 "I"s is helpful and important. I would like to suggest four other thoughts when it comes to weapons and/or a suspected or possible threat to safety.

- Err on the side of safety. Very few people will be upset with you if you are insuring the safety of their lives or their children's lives. If they are upset with you, too bad.

- Kids are smart, but you are smarter. Don't let them fool you and don't give up at first blush if you are trying to find something or get some information. Think beyond the obvious.

- Don't be super-administrator, super-teacher, or super-anything. Don't venture alone and don't take unnecessary chances. Be careful at every corner and with every step.
- "Kids will be kids" does not hold water when it comes to threats or dangerous situations. There is nothing funny about pretending to have a weapon, threatening to blow the place up, or telling someone you are going to kill them. Take these situations seriously and act appropriately.

I bet there are few teachers or administrators who have not been involved with a situation similar to this one, especially if they deal with kids in the intermediate and older ages. Many years ago we could, and did, take these things less seriously, and most of the time we were right. Not anymore. Columbine and other events have changed the way we think and the way we act, and it should also have changed the way that kids think and act, too. Kids are not oblivious to the ramifications of making threats or acting in a threatening manner, nor should we give them much leeway when they cross the line. Act fair, act quickly, but act—and then discipline.

Case Study #4: This One Has a Nice Ring to It

Tammy Teacher recently purchased a new cell phone with all the bells and whistles. The cost of the phone was over $600, but Tammy believes that the money was well spent. One morning, Tammy showed her new phone to a group of ten students who were assembled in the classroom before the start of the school day. When the bell rang signaling the beginning of first hour, Tammy placed the phone in the top drawer of her desk. Later, in that first hour, Tammy opened her top desk drawer to get a pen and noticed that the phone was missing. Tammy suspected that one of the students to whom she was talking before class stole her phone. When the bell rang to end class, Tammy required the ten "suspects" to remain. Tammy asked if anyone took the phone, but none of the students came forward. Tammy therefore conducted a massive search for the phone by searching all ten of the students and their purses, backpacks, coats, and other effects. The phone was eventually located.

Administrative Perspective:

This case study is a bit vague, so let's make a few general assumptions before we criticize Tammy Teacher. My first assumption is that Tammy is a bit light in the cranium. Who brings a $600 phone to school and puts it in her desk drawer when the bell is ringing and kids are in the room? Who buys a $600 phone in the first place? My second assumption is that there are two groups of students involved, the ten she spoke to before class and the kids in her class who may or may not have seen her put the phone away when the bell rang.

No matter, Tammy doesn't have any proof or even reasonable evidence of who it was that took the phone. She assumes it was one of the kids she showed the phone to before class, but that is more of a hunch than an evidentiary deduction. Tammy is just guessing, and, thus, she has no right to search anything or anybody based on a simple guess.

I would have done things differently. I would have asked the ten students to stop by for just a minute after school.

Then, when they came by on their own, and not because they had to, I would share with them that my phone went missing sometime after I showed it to them, and that I noticed it gone before the end of first hour. I would ask that if anyone knows anything about it, would he or she please be kind enough to help me solve the mystery. I would also tell them that I have called the police since the phone was very expensive and I learned that if anyone stole the phone he or she might be guilty of a felony. I would then proceed to call all ten of their parents and ask if they would encourage their son/daughter to talk to their friends and see if we can solve this crime outside of the police investigation, which has already been started. A little parental and peer pressure is often all you need to find the culprit—and the very expensive phone.

When a student throws a spitball at the blackboard (or is it a whiteboard or a Smartboard?), you don't keep every student after school for thirty minutes hoping someone will nark on a friend. Group punishment for the actions of one student is as wrong as group searches when you have no idea who is even a suspect.

So, Tammy, I can summarize my thoughts on this case study rather quickly. First, you have a screw loose for bringing a $600 phone to school and putting it in your desk drawer in front of a class of kids and for even showing it to kids. Next, you can't just assume someone is guilty of stealing the phone. Remember, even educators, who have more latitude than the police when it comes to solving school crimes, must have some evidence before they start conducting searches of property or persons. Finally, did you ever think of just calling the phone and listening for it to ring?

Tammy, I'm trying to tell you that you blew this one. Can you hear me, Tammy? Can you hear me now?

Legal Perspective:

I can hear you, Jim. The case certainly is vague, but, in fact, it's based on an actual situation that I am presently dealing with as I write this response. Only the names have been changed to protect the guilty. Clearly, Tammy's search methods are not ideal. My comments are therefore directed at how the situation should have been handled from a legal perspective.

The first thing that Tammy Teacher should have done is attempt to solve the mystery without engaging in a search, where the students are protected by the Fourth Amendment. To do this, Tammy could certainly call the phone to see which student starts ringing or vibrating. (After all, how many of us have done this to locate our own cell phones that we misplaced!) Tammy could also ask the remaining students if she can search their bags or purses or whatever before they leave, in order to eliminate them as suspects. If a student consents to the search, it is not protected by the Fourth Amendment. However, note that in trying these methods, Tammy can only detain the students for a reasonable amount of time. If Tammy requires the students to remain for too long, it may implicate Fourth Amendment seizure concerns.

Assuming that calling the phone and searching the students who consent do not turn up the phone, Tammy should determine if she has reasonable suspicion to conduct a search of the remaining students by examining the four "I"s of inception. (Let me discuss these in a slightly different order.)

Nature of the infraction: I would say that the infraction here is not overly serious. We are not looking for a weapon or drugs. Although theft is a somewhat serious infraction, the cell phone can be replaced and no permanent damage will result if the phone is never located.

Informant information: Here, we have absolutely no informant information. No student has come forward to provide relevant information.

Individual suspicion: Likewise, we have relatively weak individual suspicion. We have a group of suspects, as opposed to a single suspect.

Intrusiveness of the place to be searched: The instant search would hopefully start with student backpacks and purses, but could quickly lead to a search of the students themselves.

Based on the above, I do not believe that there is reasonable suspicion to search any or all of the student suspects. The closer the search gets to the students themselves, the weaker the case becomes. I believe that Tammy needs to bolster the informant information by talking individually to the students in the class to determine if anyone saw anything suspicious. Second, Tammy needs to narrow the field of potential suspects. If these two things can be successfully done, there may be reasonable suspicion to conduct a search. If not, Tammy may need to eat the cost of buying a new phone.

In closing, two points are critical to make. First, if reasonable suspicion does exist to search a student, the search must also be reasonable in scope. Here, the searcher may only look in those places that it is reasonable to believe that the missing cell phone might be found. Also, Tammy must be careful that her search is not overly aggressive. A search where students are required to have private areas of their bodies examined is significantly overbroad when it comes to searching for a missing cell phone.

Second, and equally as important, the fact that Tammy Teacher eventually found the phone in the above scenario is absolutely irrelevant to whether or not the search was conducted properly. Sure, Tammy will get to keep her phone, but the manner in which the phone was recovered will probably make it impossible to punish the thief, as improperly obtained evidence can generally not be used as a basis for discipline. Additionally, Tammy may personally be liable for civil damages sought by parents of the students who were illegally and improperly searched.

“Remember that our nation’s
great leaders were also
our first great scholars.”

John F. Kennedy

Chapter Four

Student Discipline for Off-Campus Misconduct: Hey, Get Out of MySpace!

Brian D. Schwartz

Introduction

It often seems that parents, community members, shopkeepers, civic organizations, and others expect the local public school district to deal with every student "issue," even when the event in question occurred completely away from school. For example, how many times have you, the reader, received an email from a student's parent expecting you to intervene in a dispute that occurred at the local shopping mall on a Saturday afternoon? Or, how often have you received a phone call from a community member expecting you to discipline "one of your students" for conduct that occurred on a day that school was not in session?

The problem at hand has only become worse with the advent of technology. Frequently, students use email, instant messaging, texting, MySpace, and other online resources to fight, bully, harass, demean, threaten, cajole, entice, allure, persuade, and beguile other students. And, yes, sometimes these tools of the devil are even used for purposes of good over evil; however, as any school official will tell you, this is generally not the case!

The purpose of this chapter is therefore to examine in detail the ability of a public school district to discipline students for events that occur wholly off-campus and away from school. What we will discover is that school districts and school officials have more power and discretion than one might think.

On-Campus versus Off-Campus

Before proceeding, it is important to distinguish between what constitutes on-campus and what is considered off-campus. The definition of on-campus is generally fairly broad and encompasses more than just the physical property of the school district and its proximity. In most jurisdictions, students who are at a local eatery during open campus lunch, at an away basketball game, on a field trip, or waiting at the bus stop are considered to be on-campus for purposes of the school district being able to regulate student conduct.

The language sometimes used by school districts to extend the long arm of on-campus discipline is "portal to portal." This literally means that the school district can discipline students as if they were on campus from the moment they leave their home to go to school to the moment they reach home after school. However, it must be noted that this disciplinary scheme assumes that students proceed directly from their home to school and then directly from school back home again. Certainly, if a student varies his or her route—such as stopping by a friend's house on the way home—this breaks the sequence of events for the purpose of being able to discipline a student as if he or she is on campus.

Off-Campus Discipline in General

Many times, however, student conduct truly takes place off-campus. The question thus arises as to whether school districts can impose disciplinary consequences for such off-campus behavior. This very question peaked the national interest in 2003 when a group of high school-age girls from Illinois were disciplined for an off-campus brawl.

In *Gendelman v. Glenbrook North High School*, certain members of the Glenbrook North High School's junior and senior class met for an annual "powder puff" football game. The gathering took place on a Sunday in the Cook County Forest Preserve, Chippilly Woods. The event was anything but a game, with girls from the senior class hazing girls from the junior class. Days after the event, the school's administration disciplined several of the students for, in part, violating the student handbook's rules prohibiting hazing and harassment. Two of the students who were disciplined challenged the authority of the school district in federal district court, claiming that their actions took place outside the purview of the school and therefore they could not be suspended or otherwise disciplined by school officials.

The court, however, sided with the school district and upheld the disciplinary consequences. As for the students' argument that the event occurred off-campus and beyond the reach of the school, the court found a sufficient connection to the school to allow school officials to act. In particular, the court pointed to the fact that "attendance…and class standing were essential to the roles played" by the students. Further, the court alluded to the fact that the event was planned and organized at the school. Given these factors, the court found that school officials had authority to impose disciplinary consequences.

The above case is illustrative of the majority of court decisions regarding a school or district's ability to discipline students for purely off-campus misconduct. The key questions that most courts examine in determining whether or not discipline can be imposed are as follows.

Has the student violated a school rule or school district policy?

Is there a "nexus" or sufficient connection between the off-campus misconduct and the school?

From a due process perspective, the first question is extremely important. Students must be placed on notice of expected behavior and the consequences for violating the code of conduct. Hence, school officials must point to a specific handbook rule or school district policy that the student violated in order to invoke discipline. To this end, it is further recommended that rules and policies specifically include language allowing school officials to discipline students for off-campus conduct that bears a reasonable relationship to the school.

The requirement that the off-campus misconduct bear a connection back to the school is somewhat difficult to understand. This requires school officials to demonstrate more than just a causal relationship between the student and the school. The fact that the individual who committed the offense is a student at the school is not sufficient. Rather, school officials must show some tangible connection between the off-campus misconduct and the operations of the school. The case discussed above provides an excellent example of this requirement. Here, the off-campus brawl was planned at school and the role each student played was based on whether the student was a junior or senior.

In terms of another example, consider the following: On a warm summer day (when school is not in session), a teacher and her former student see each other at a local grocery store. The teacher politely says hello to the student, who responds by throwing an apple at the teacher. In this case, the school would probably be prohibited from disciplining the student. The situation happened when school was not in session and the student's reaction to the teacher did not extend directly from the student-teacher relationship. Now suppose that the above event occurred shortly after the conclusion of a school day and only hours after this very teacher had assigned this very student a detention. Here, provided that the student violated a school rule by his conduct, a nexus or relationship between the student's conduct and the school can most likely be established.

Another way that the nexus or tangible connection can occur is if the student's misconduct begins on school grounds but is then continued or completed off-campus. Several courts have upheld discipline in cases where students made verbal threats to each other at school and later fought off-campus. Likewise, a court in Pennsylvania let stand a suspension where a student agreed to sell drugs at school, even though the transaction was later completed at an off-campus location.

It is also important to remember that the school district bears the burden of establishing the connection between the student's off-campus misconduct and the school. It is therefore important for school officials to meticulously document both the school rule that was violated and the connection or nexus between the off-campus misconduct and the school.

Student Free Speech and Off-Campus Discipline

As discussed in the introduction to this chapter, the advent of modern technology has led to an entirely new venue for off-campus student communication. And sometimes the problems that develop through these communications come to roost the next day at school! In the cases that we have examined thus far, we have not discussed student conduct that enters the realm of student speech, which may be protected under the First Amendment.

Because student communications may be protected by the First Amendment, courts require something *extra* before school officials can discipline students for off-campus speech. In addition to a violation of a school rule and a nexus or tangible connection between the student's conduct and the school, courts require that school officials document an exception to free speech. These exceptions to free speech are discussed in detail in Chapter 2 and delineate cases where the courts have allowed school districts to prohibit student speech and expression. Generally, the exceptions to free speech that are applicable to off-campus communications are as follows: speech that is materially and substantially disruptive to the school setting, speech that creates a safety concern at the school, and speech that constitutes a true threat.

Hence, the test for school officials to consider before disciplining students for off-campus behavior that constitutes speech is as follows:

- Has the student violated a school rule or school district policy?
- Is there a "nexus" or sufficient connection between the off-campus misconduct and the school?
- Is there an exception to free speech?

In applying this expanded three-prong test to off-campus speech, school officials should take great care to fully investigate and document the student misconduct. There have been cases where students have been disciplined for off-campus speech and courts have reversed the disciplinary decision of the school because the investigating school official did not have the full story before taking action.

Take, for example, an early off-campus Internet discipline case out of Missouri. In 1998, a Missouri student developed a website entirely on his home computer that referred to school staff with vulgar language and invited viewers of the website to express their own thoughts on school personnel. After being disciplined by school officials, the student brought suit against the school district claiming a violation of his First Amendment rights. The court found for the student, holding that school officials had failed to show (under the *Tinker* standard) that the student's website caused a material and substantial disruption to the school setting. The fact that school officials disliked the content of the website and were upset was alone insufficient to overcome the student's First Amendment rights.

In another case out of Washington in 2000, a student created an "unofficial" school website. The website was designed and maintained totally off-campus and included mock obituaries of students and a ballot where viewers could vote for who should die next. As with the above case, the student sued after he was disciplined by the school district. At the trial, the student presented evidence that the idea for the website came from his English class, where students where given an assignment to write a mock obituary. The court found that absent a "true threat" the school district could not discipline the student for his actions.

In contrast to the above cases, courts have upheld student discipline for off-campus websites and off-campus Internet speech in the following cases: (1) a student solicited donations to kill a teacher, (2) a student invited viewers of his website to post death threats against teachers, (3) a student established a ranking system for female students at the school in accordance with who had the "best booty," and (4) a student created a fake page on MySpace depicting her principal as a pedophile and a sex addict.

In examining the above cases, it appears certain that courts want to see substantial evidence regarding the third-prong of the off-campus discipline test, mainly firm evidence that the situation has been fully investigated and that the student's speech or expression is subject to restriction. Remember, in these cases we might be dealing with enhanced student constitutional rights. Before taking action, courts want to make sure that school officials get *all* the facts and get them correctly!

24-7-365 Athletic Conduct Codes and Student Discipline

Students clearly do not have a constitutional right to participate in athletics and extracurricular activities. As a result, many school districts have adopted strict athletic codes of conduct that impose restrictions on a student's ability to participate in sports and other extracurricular activities if he or she fails to adhere to certain expectations, even while off-campus. These expectations, as we will see below, mainly prohibit students from using or possessing alcohol, tobacco, and illegal drugs.

Some of these athletic codes have been dubbed "24-7-365" policies due to the fact that they impose a code of conduct 24 hours a day, 7 days a week, and 365 days a year. As we begin to look at these athletic code policies, it is important to note that they should apply only to a student's ability to participate in athletics and extracurricular activities. A school cannot generally impose academic or disciplinary consequences for a violation of a 24-7-365 athletic policy.

A somewhat common 24-7-365 policy might look something like this:

Except for supervised medications prescribed by a physician, a student under the influence, using, possessing, buying, or receiving tobacco in any form, drugs and look-alike drugs, anabolic steroids, controlled substances, and alcohol at any time and at any place is in violation of the athletic code and, if apprehended by school or appropriate law enforcement personnel, is subject to the following consequences:

First Violation:...
Second Violation:...
Subsequent Violations:...

This policy will be in effect during the entire calendar year, inclusive of all training, conditioning, practices, and other school related/sponsored activities. This policy remains in effect 24 hours a day, 7 days a week, 365 days a year.

In looking at the example above, a few points are worth making. First, it should be noted that the students are prohibited from being under the influence, using, possessing, buying, or receiving drugs, alcohol, and other banned substances. Many policies that we have reviewed only prohibit students from being under the influence of the banned substances. Such a policy is not nearly expansive enough and would tie the hands of school officials in imposing discipline.

Second, the above policy only allows students to be disciplined if they are apprehended by school or appropriate law enforcement personnel. Many policies that we have reviewed do not distinguish how information of wrongdoing is obtained. For example, the mother of the student who did not make the cheerleading team could bring in cell phone pictures showing the cheerleading team captain drinking at a party on a Saturday night. We do not discourage such broad policies, but only caution that school officials should conduct a full investigation to verify that the evidence is trustworthy and accurately portrayed.

Third, it should be noted that many 24-7-365 policies, including the sample policy above, are in effect even during the off-season. There has been some debate in the legal and education community as to whether or not a school district can impose athletic disciplinary consequences during the off-season or when a student is not playing a sport. The critics of such a policy have opined that during the off-season the student is not an athlete. School officials are encouraged to consult with their own legal counsel on this issue.

Conclusion

School officials can generally discipline students for off-campus misconduct if it can be shown that this conduct violated a school rule or district policy and there is a connection or nexus between the off-campus conduct and the school. Perhaps the greatest number and most serious of infractions concerned the Internet. While the Internet is a tremendous resource for students to learn and expand their horizons, it is also a tool for students to communicate with others in a way that is not always appropriate. When students engage in misconduct that constitutes speech, whether through the Internet or other means, school officials must also show an exception to such speech before a student can be disciplined for his or her off-campus misconduct. School officials are strongly reminded to document, document, and document their findings!

Case Study #5:
Superintendent Sides Decides

Superintendent Sides arrives at the school district office one morning and is confronted by a parent who has "an emergency." The parent shows Dr. Sides one of several emails that were sent to her daughter Melanie by another student Lanie. The emails, which were sent and received during non-school hours, are both vulgar and threatening. One email, in particular, threatens to beat up Melanie if she tries out for the cheerleading squad. The parent is adamant that the school district deal with this situation.

Legal Perspective:

When student misconduct takes place truly off-campus, a school district is limited in its ability to intercede. As discussed in the chapter text, the key in determining whether or not school officials can take disciplinary action involves an analysis under a three-prong test. Here, school officials must determine (1) whether the student violated a school rule or district policy, (2) if there is a nexus or relationship between the off-campus misconduct and the school, and (3) in cases of student speech, whether there is an exception to free speech.

In this particular situation, Superintendent Sides should ask for copies of all the email correspondence to begin her investigation. For the purpose of my response, I will assume that Superintendent Sides handles this situation herself. Jim might argue that the superintendent should refer the matter to the building level administrator.

At the onset, it is absolutely critical that Superintendent Sides verify that the emails were actually sent by Lanie. With today's technology, this can no longer be assumed. Recently, there have been many high profile incidents of cyberbullying where the individual first accused of wrongdoing was actually not involved in the misconduct. Identifying the aggressor is essential and can be done with the help of the technology director and also by talking to Lanie and other students. I'm sure that Jim will have some good practical advice in dealing with Lanie and in conducting interviews of those who may have information or otherwise be involved in this situation.

Assuming that it can be proven that Lanie did indeed send the emails, we can turn our attention to the three-prong, off-campus discipline test. With respect to the first element, showing a violation of policy, it's reasonable to assume that most schools, at the very least, have a rule prohibiting bullying. Superintendent Sides should, however, seek to identify *all* the school policies that the student has violated. This is important should one specific policy violation fall short in a subsequent school board hearing or court case.

The second prong of the test, establishing a nexus or relationship back to the school, can be difficult. Remember, it is important to show a connection between the school and the actual off-campus conduct. It is not enough to simply establish that the girls are both students in the district. In this case, some questions to ask might include:

Were the emails sent in response to an incident that started at school? (Remember, one of the emails talked about the cheerleading squad.)

Did Melanie and Lanie have any arguments, fights, or disagreements at school in the days immediately preceding the emails?

Are there any documented cases of disagreements between Lanie and Melanie while they were at school?

Since the emails were sent, have there been any arguments or altercations between Melanie and Lanie while at school?

Were school district computers or email addresses used in any way in the transmission or receipt of the emails?

Has the superintendent or any other school official had to spend a significant amount of time dealing with this situation?

If there have been previous incidents between the two girls at school or if the matter with the emails spilled over into school, a nexus or relationship between the off-campus misconduct and the school can probably be established. Likewise, if school computers or emails were used in any way, school officials will have little difficulty proving a nexus. Some jurisdictions have also allowed a nexus to be created if school officials were required to dedicate a significant amount of their time in dealing with an off-campus student situation.

Lastly, because we may be dealing with a First Amendment issue, school officials are required to document one of the exceptions to free speech. As you will remember from the chapter text, these are situations where free speech either does not apply or can be regulated by the school district. In this case, the emails that Lanie sent may constitute a true threat or a safety concern. Because the comments were made privately in an email, the school district probably cannot hang its hat on the fact that the speech may have been vulgar, lewd, or obscene. Likewise, because of the private context in which the comments were made, the school district probably cannot immediately show a material and substantial disruption to the educational setting. This, of course, can change if Melanie and Lanie bring their disagreement into the schoolhouse and engage in disruptive behavior.

This three-prong test does not, however, end our analysis. Superintendent Sides must also do her homework to assure that the emails are really of a serious and threatening nature. In doing so, it is critical to show that Melanie really felt threatened or apprehensive about trying out for the cheerleading squad as a result of Lanie's emails. If Melanie was not nearly as upset as her mother, discipline of Lanie may not be appropriate.

Lastly, if Superintendent Sides does decide that the school district cannot discipline Lanie, there are still steps that she can take to attempt to assist in this situation. For instance, it would be perfectly appropriate for the Superintendent and the school district counselor or other school officials to talk to both girls, either together or individually, to address the situation. Also, if the situation is sufficiently serious, it would be appropriate for Superintendent Sides to refer Melanie's mother to local law enforcement officials.

Administrative Perspective:

Nice Job, Brian. As usual, you have made my job easy.

Let me begin by saying that this case study does truly represent many similar ones that administrators will face during their sentence as school judge, jury, and legal consultants for every side of every issue. And, speaking of sides, Superintendent Sides has been given some great suggestions by Barrister Brian!

I agree that step number one in this case is to collect the data. The parent's concern rests entirely on the emails in question. Superintendent Sides must not only retain hard copies of these emails, but must inquire if there are more from recent situations or situations in the past. Any email that may lend credence to the stated concerns should be turned over for consideration.

Once Inspector/Superintendent Sides determines that thc emails require further probing, I would suggest the most prudent and direct form of data gathering would be a direct interrogation of the two “lanies”: Lanie and Melanie. Brian has already suggested two pertinent lines of questioning for both young ladies. First, I would see just how upset Melanie is with the alleged threats. She may, in fact, not be fazed at all by her “friend’s” comments, and she may consider this to simply be a teenage conversation blown out of context by parents. To Melanie this may be a short-term misunderstanding already replaced with BFF emails and all sorts of cryptic coding between two friends. Shamefully, we all know that many (but not all) kids communicate in lewd, inappropriate, and vulgar conversation. It seems that there must be an “800” number kids can call if parents threaten, or God forbid, actually engage in mouth washing these days. I know I risk aging myself by saying this, but if I used the language many kids use these days, my cholesterol count would be 40% Ivory.

If Melanie is upset, frightened, or feels truly threatened by her abbreviated friendship with Lanie, we then need to continue with the investigation. Another consideration we must think about is that Melanie may indeed feign a cavalier attitude about the entire incident in an effort to cover her true fear of the consequences of getting Lanie in trouble. This is where we use our intuition and sixth sense while we process the responses of our interviews. Sometimes “gut” feelings preside over actual verbiage.

If, indeed, Melanie convinces us that this caper is just nasty teenage angst and not a serious threat or involved issue, I would assume Superintendent Sides will circle the troops and try to negotiate some form of resolution, bringing the crisis to a grinding halt with cries of "yippee" being heard from the super's office when all depart for the hinterlands.

Brian also outlines six other considerations that must be investigated by Inspector Sides in determining if there is a nexus between emails and the school. These six questions may answer one or more steps on the three-prong test. I would even add another question to the list. "Was there any discussion, problem, or situation with any members of the cheerleading team that might be related to the so-called 'threat'?" Other students may hold the key to the alleged threat which may, or may not, be directly related to the Lanie and Melanie relationship. For instance, Lanie may not want Melanie to try out because there is a chance that Kelanie won't make the team, and the threat is really coming from Kelanie, via Lanie, to Melanie. (Couldn't one of these kids be named Barbara?)

Brian wondered if Superintendent Sides was the right person to conduct the investigation. Good question. Since the parent went to her, the investigation rightly belongs to her. She may defer it to a building administrator, athletic director, or central office administrator depending on the size and organization of the district—and that would be appropriately the decision of Ms. Sides. I won't speculate on this decision other than to say that if she passes the question to another administrator, I would hope she would do it immediately and preferably in the presence of the parent. I would also hope that Superintendent Sides would gratefully thank the parent for seeking assistance from the school and offer assurance that if there are any questions about the resolution, She is more than willing to talk about them. In other words, give the parent a speedy response to the request for help, a kind thank you, and a willingness to assist further if needed. Quality Service 101 at work.

I would also like to agree with Brian's valid suggestion that the administration continues to search for related violations other than the obvious. In this case, inappropriate language, misuse of school technology, and engaging bullying or threatening behaviors are the obvious violations. It is also possible that further investigation may reveal other significant issues. I found that while I investigated specific situations it was helpful to keep a log of possible issues that might be underlying or adjacent to the obvious. As discussions unfold, these "hidden" violations have a way of surfacing. Keeping an open mind to variations on the thread of evidence is often helpful in finding the real reasons for the issues at hand. Another good suggestion shared with me early in my career was to run the facts and findings by a third party for a less prejudiced viewpoint. At different times in my years as an educator, I was lucky enough to develop some fine relationships with law officials (lawyers and police officers), and sometimes I would call or visit them briefly and discuss a list of "what-ifs" in my investigation. Often they were able to open my eyes or refocus them in new directions.

No matter what Superintendent Sides discovers, I agree with Brian that, at the very least, a discussion of ***what is right*** needs to be conducted with the girls and/or parents, coaches, and adults involved. At the very minimum, language issues and appropriate use of technology seem to be open for discussion. Let's also be sure to give kudos to the parent for taking steps to solve this communication caper, if indeed the intent was just and proper.

Finally, when issues like this raise their ugly head, administrators—who may be sinking in the minutia of NCLB, standardized tests, budgets, contracts, lunch menus, wayward employees, and over-zealous citizens—should recognize that when a parent walks in with an issue like this, it is top priority to the families involved and must be treated with due respect and diligence. This is not always easy to do when the clock only allows 24 hours per day.

I have one last point. Brian might differ with what I am about to say; however, I doubt it. I never let things like "prongs" decide, entirely, how I responded to real concerns. If a kid is truly being threatened, or if two kids are truly engaged in vulgar, lewd, and inappropriate conversations, and the mom or dad needs help to sort things out and solve the situation, then we need to do everything we can to help. Whether or not we find a nexus or a Lexus in the process was never what motivated me to solve the problem. I truly do understand that if we get sucked into a legal battle, we may lose if we don't do our due diligence at every fork in the road, but honestly, most situations are solved long before the gavel is lowered and the balances of justice are recalculated. Finding Middle Ground and viable solutions are what motivates us to do our jobs well.

Chapter Five

Educational Issues Regarding Homeschool Students: Return of the Jedi

Brian D. Schwartz

Introduction

In 1925, the United States Supreme Court emphatically declared that parents have options in directing the educational upbringing of their children. Specifically, in *Pierce v. Society of Sisters of the Holy Names of Jesus and Mary*, the Court held that states can require that children receive an education, but they cannot compel attendance in the public school system. This opened the door to parents educating their children in a variety of ways, including private schools and home-based schools.

The United States Department of Education's Center for Education Statistics estimates that in 2003, there were approximately 1.1 million students who were homeschooled in the United States. This number represents a staggering 2.2 percent of the entire school-age population at that time. Based on past trends, it is estimated that over 1.4 million children were homeschooled in the United States in 2007 and that as many as 1.8 million students could be home-educated in 2010.

Although no statistical research exists, it is safe to say that each year a significant number of homeschool students and families seek services from their local public school system. The services requested vary from the use of textbooks to part-time attendance to participation in athletics and other activities.

Currently, twenty states mandate by law or administrative rule that privately educated students receive some degree of access to public school services. These states are Arizona, Colorado, Florida, Idaho, Illinois, Iowa, Maine, Massachusetts, Michigan, Minnesota, Nevada, New Hampshire, North Dakota, Oregon, Pennsylvania, Tennessee, Utah, Vermont, Washington, and Wyoming. However, the exact services that are made available in the above states differ dramatically. For the states listed above, readers should consult legal counsel when addressing questions regarding the ability of homeschool students to access public school services.

The majority of states, however, make no provision for services to homeschool students. In these states, the question therefore arises as to whether or not homeschool students are entitled to access any services from their local public school system. From a legal perspective, almost all courts have ruled against homeschool families who have filed lawsuits to compel their local public school district to provide services not otherwise required by law, rule, or policy. A number of public school systems do, however, voluntarily provide services to homeschool students.

This chapter seeks to explore situations where homeschool students and their families seek services from the public schools located within their jurisdiction. In particular, we will examine the loaning of textbooks and other curricular material, part-time attendance, athletic and extracurricular participation, testing and placement, class rank and graduation, and special education services.

Textbooks and Curricular Material

It is clear that a state or local public school district may share textbooks and curricular material with homeschools and other nonpublic schools within their jurisdiction. However, unless otherwise provided by law, homeschools and nonpublic schools do not have an absolute right to receive these materials from the local public school system.

It must be stressed that local public school districts providing textbooks and other services to nonpublic schools on a voluntary basis should be careful to ensure that this act of benevolence does not otherwise run afoul of the law, especially in cases where home and nonpublic schools engage in discriminatory practices or are deeply entrenched in religion. The United States Supreme Court has stated that local public school districts are prohibited from providing aid to private schools and homeschools that discriminate based on race, sex, and other constitutional factors. Accordingly, public school districts must assure non-discriminatory practices by any nonpublic schools that are provided services.

Additionally, local school districts wishing to provide textbooks and other aid to home and nonpublic schools must ensure that their actions do not violate the Establishment Clause of the First Amendment. In *Lemon v. Kurtzman*, the United States Supreme Court considered whether state reimbursement to private schools violated the First Amendment. Specifically, the Court examined a Pennsylvania law allowing the state to reimburse nonpublic schools (which were mostly Catholic) for teacher salaries, instructional material, and textbooks. At the same time, the Court looked at a Rhode Island law supplementing salaries at nonpublic elementary schools by 15 percent. As in Pennsylvania, most of these funds were spent on Catholic schools.

The Court set up the now famous "*Lemon* test," a three-prong approach used to determine whether public aid to private schools is permissible under the First Amendment. Under this test (1) the government's action must have a legitimate secular purpose, (2) the government's action must not have the primary effect of either advancing or inhibiting religion, and (3) the government's action must not result in an excessive government entanglement with religion. In applying this test, the Court invalidated both the Pennsylvania and Rhode Island statutes.

Lastly, local public school districts seeking to voluntarily give aid to home and nonpublic schools should ensure that the provision of such aid does not violate provisions of their state's constitution. For example, the Supreme Court of Missouri found that aid to private school districts violated the Missouri constitutional provision providing that "neither the general assembly nor any other governmental unit may make an appropriation or pay from any public fund whatsoever anything in aid of any religious creed, church, or sectarian purpose." However, the Supreme Court of Nebraska found that the loan of textbooks to students in private schools did not violate the state's constitutional provision prohibiting the appropriation of public funds to nonpublic schools.

Part-time Attendance

Homeschool parents frequently request enrollment of their children in one or two classes at the appropriate local public school. According to the United States Department of Education's National Center for Education Statistics, approximately 198,000 homeschool students were enrolled part-time in the public school system in 2003. Although there is no statistical research on the reason that homeschool families seek these services from the public school system, it can be presumed that the homeschool does not have the time, resources, or specialized skills to provide a particular type of instruction.

Absent a state statute to the contrary, public school districts have, however, frequently opposed allowing homeschool students the right to attend academic classes on a part-time basis, as there is often no mechanism for counting these students for the purpose of receiving state aid. The decision to disallow part-time attendance has generally been upheld by courts where no statutory right to part-time attendance otherwise exists.

Athletic and Extracurricular Activities

Another hotly contested issue concerns the ability of homeschool students to participate in extracurricular activities and to try out for athletic teams within their local public school district. With respect to athletics, the public schools of most states fall under the jurisdiction of a state athletic association or other similar governing body. Absent a state law or policy of the state's athletic association, school districts have been victorious in almost all cases where homeschool parents have sued, demanding that their children be allowed to participate in sports and other extracurricular events. A majority of these decisions turn on the fact that the ability of any student to participate in athletics and other extracurricular activities is a privilege, as opposed to a property right.

In states where homeschool student athletic participation is within a school district's discretion, special consideration must be given before enacting a policy allowing for athletic participation by homeschool students. As an unanticipated consequence of its decision to allow athletic participation by homeschool students, the local public school system may be giving the homeschool athlete "credit" for work done at the homeschool. For example, the Illinois High School Association allows each member school district to determine for itself whether or not resident homeschool students are allowed to participate in athletics. However, by accepting a homeschool student, the public school district is obligated to ensure that the student is taking a minimum of twenty credit hours.

Furthermore, in accordance with the state's "no-pass, no-play" law, the public school where the homeschool student is participating in athletics must ensure that the student is maintaining a specific grade point average or a specific minimum grade in certain classes. Taken together, the association policy and state law may allow a homeschool student to successfully argue that he or she is entitled to a high school diploma from the public school if it "approves" enough credits during the time the student participated in athletics.

Testing and Placement

Another area of concern arises when former homeschool students enroll or re-enroll full-time in the public school system. The question often arises as to the appropriate grade level placement for these students. Especially in states where homeschools are minimally regulated and the curriculum may be drastically different from that of the public school system, placing the former homeschool student in the age appropriate grade is not always an acceptable option. Additionally, in states with laws prohibiting social promotion, age appropriate placement may violate the law. This is not to say that homeschool students do not perform at grade level. Frequently, it is the case where the homeschool student's preparation has propelled the student significantly above that of his or her age appropriate peers. In either event, it is incumbent upon the public school districts to adopt a policy reserving the right to perform assessment tests to determine each student's correct grade level placement.

In reserving the right to test homeschool students, public school districts should be cautious of equal protection concerns. When placing students, it is generally acceptable for a school district to accept transcripts and grades from an accredited public or private school, while reserving the right to test students coming from non-accredited schools. However, it must be noted that in doing so a public school district would be obligated to accept transcripts and grades from a homeschool that is fully accredited.

Class Rank and High School Graduation

Many students who are homeschooled throughout their entire academic career seek enrollment in the public school system around age 15 or 16 in order to graduate from the public school system and obtain a high school diploma from a state-accredited institution. This may be done, if for no other reason than to better the student's chances of gaining admission to an institution of higher education. However, it should also be noted that several public colleges are now accepting homeschool students based on homeschool grades and standardized test scores.

Although there are no significant cases on point, it appears clear that public school districts can establish uniform criteria that students must meet before they are eligible to receive a high school diploma from the district or before being given a class rank. In establishing requirements for a high school diploma or class rank, a school district is generally allowed to require that a minimum number of credits are completed at the school. Additionally, as with testing and placement procedures, a school district may allow credits taken at another accredited state or out-of-state school to count toward graduation or class rank requirements, but refuse to count credits from a non-accredited school. Again, in doing so, a public school district would be obligated to accept credits from a homeschool that is fully accredited.

Special Education Services

In looking at special education services available to homeschool students, an examination of both federal and state law is necessary. At the federal level, the 2004 reauthorization of the Individuals with Disabilities Education Act (IDEA) was greatly expanded to assure that local school districts provide equitable participation opportunities to parentally placed private school children with disabilities. The local school district where the private school is located is responsible for administering services to parentally placed private school children, including the obligation to identify, evaluate, and spend a proportionate share of federal funds on equitable services for children with disabilities. It is important to note, however, that a parentally placed private school child with disabilities does not have an individual right to receive special education and related services. The law only requires that parentally placed private school children, as a whole or group, receive a proportionate amount of services based on the ratio of private school children with disabilities compared with the number of students with disabilities in the public school district.

The definition of "private school" within IDEA does not, however, include homeschools, and federal dollars cannot be spent on students who are educated under a state law specific to homeschools. Therefore, if a state has a specific statute providing for homeschools, students are not eligible for special education services funded with federal IDEA dollars. However, in those states that do not have a specific statute governing homeschools or in situations where parents choose to homeschool their children under a state statute regulating private schools, special education services are generally available to homeschool students to the same extent as they are available to other parentally placed private school children.

The above analysis only applies to a state's expenditures of federal IDEA funds. The vast majority of special education funding in every state comes from state appropriations. Here, state governments are essentially free to spend these dollars in any way they choose. While some states specifically provide for special education services to homeschool students, most do not.

It is important to note, however, that in states that do not have a homeschool option and therefore treat homeschools as private schools, there is an obligation to provide homeschool students with the same special education services as those received by special needs students in private schools.

Conclusion

In conclusion, it is important to remember that several states mandate that public schools provide certain services to homeschool students located within their boundaries. In states that do not address this topic by law or administrative rule, public school districts are generally free to offer homeschool families a variety of services on a part-time or "cafeteria style" basis.

However, in cases where homeschool parents have sued local public school districts mandating that services be provided, these lawsuits have generally failed. Public schools can generally enact "you're in or you're out" policies, whereby students must be enrolled on a full-time basis in order to receive services.

The one exception to the above assertions may be in the area of special education services. In determining the accessibility of services, it is first necessary to look at federal law to determine if a homeschool student is being educated under a homeschool specific statute or a statute governing private schools in general. If the homeschool child is being educated under a homeschool specific statute, federal funds cannot be used to provide special education services. If the child is being educated under a private school statute, special education services are generally made available; however, there is still no individual entitlement to these services.

States are free to expend state special education funds in virtually any way the state deems appropriate. Again, in states without a homeschool specific statute, homeschool and private school students must be treated the same in terms of special education services that are made available. However, in states with a homeschool specific statute, states may deny homeschool students access to any and all special education services.

Case Study #6:
The Brader Bunch

Carol and Mike Brader have six children, all homeschooled. On the first day of the school year, the Braders show up at the local public school district seeking services for three of their children, as follows: (1) Greg is sixteen and the Braders want him enrolled full-time as a high school junior, (2) Jan is thirteen and the parents want her enrolled part-time in music and advanced algebra, and (3) Bobby is ten and for him they are seeking special education services.

Legal Perspective:

Wow, the Braders sure do have a bunch of kids.

As noted in the chapter text, the services the local public school district is obligated to provide depend mainly on state specific law. There are, however, some general legal comments that can be made about a local public school system's responsibility to deal with homeschool families. I'm sure that Jim will also have a great deal of practical advice on this matter.

Let's take Greg first. Statistics show that a significant number of homeschooled children seek to enroll in the local public school system around age sixteen in order to complete public school and receive a high school diploma. To the extent that the family lives in the school district where they are seeking enrollment, Greg must be enrolled as a full-time student. This would be true even if Greg showed up in the middle of the school term.

Statistics also show that homeschools vary widely in the quality of education that they provide. Some sixteen-year-old homeschool students are perfectly prepared to step into public school at the same grade as their age appropriate peers. Other homeschool students are dreadfully ill prepared to enter into a classroom with students of their same age. Because of this fact, it is critical that the local public school system—by policy—reserve the right to administer standardized placement tests to homeschool students.

In developing a policy regarding the school district's ability to provide placement tests to homeschool students, it is critical to note that all students who enroll in the district for the first time must be treated with some uniformity. I like a policy where the local school district accepts academic credits from another public or private accredited school when determining placement, but reserves the right to test all children who do not transfer from an accredited institution.

In the case at hand, Greg should be administered standardized placement tests to see where he fits academically. If Greg performs low for his age, the school district has a couple of options in handling the situation. One option is to simply place Greg at the grade level that he fits academically. The second option is to place Greg in the age appropriate grade and provide supplemental services to help Greg catch up. In large part, this decision depends on how far Greg is behind his peers.

It is also possible that Greg will test extremely high. In fact, Greg may test so high that at the end of his high school experience he may be the top student in the class academically. In these cases, it is important to remember that a local public school district has the ability to place reasonable and uniform restrictions on class rank and graduation requirements. Here, Greg could be required to complete a certain number of credits in the district before being eligible for class rank and other awards or a high school diploma.

Now, let's turn our attention to Jan, who is seeking part-time enrollment for music and algebra. Here, it is important to see the law of your particular state. Some states have statutory provisions mandating part-time services. For example, Illinois, where Jim and I are from, mandates that homeschool students receive driver's education from their local public school district, but largely leaves the decisions regarding enrollment in other classes up to the individual district.

In states without statutory or regulatory guidance, local public school districts can generally—by policy—choose whether or not to enroll homeschool students on a part-time basis. However, this decision must treat all students with parity. For example, it would be permissible for a local school district to enact a policy stating that homeschool students will only be allowed to enroll in those classes where there is room after full-time student enrollment has been determined. However, it would certainly be improper to pick and choose which homeschool students are admitted based on such factors as family dynamics.

Our last student seeking services is Bobby, who the Braders believe is in need of special education services. If Bobby is only suspected of having a disability, the local public school district is probably obligated to provide testing to Bobby. However, if Bobby is found to be in need of special education services, federal law does not necessarily guarantee such services. Remember, a homeschool child with disabilities does not have an individual right to receive special education and related services. The law only requires that parentally placed private school children, as a whole or group, must receive a proportionate amount of services.

To further complicate matters, federal law does not include homeschooled children within the definition of those who are eligible for services. Hence, if a state has a specific statute governing homeschools, homeschool students are not eligible to receive services funded with federal dollars. If, however, the state does not have a specific statute governing homeschools or the parents are educating their child under a general state statute regulating private schools, homeschool students—as a group—are eligible for services. Each state, however, has significant latitude in expending state funds in any way it deems appropriate.

Administrative Perspective:

The Brader Family has homeschooled their little darlings for many years, and all of a sudden they see a few cracks in the armor of the wonders of home education. Mom doesn't know what to do with Bobby who is displaying some characteristics or behaviors consistent with a learning disability. Jan wants to take music and that is not one of the courses offered in the kitchen classroom, and both mom and dad are not whiz kids in math, so the advanced math thing is beyond their scope as well. Greg is 16, wants to drive, has possibly discovered that the prospects of dating some babe are a bit stifled in the confines of the home-based school and maybe, just maybe, he wants to play baseball with more than the after-school group of neighbors, who range in age from 10-14. I may be way off base in my assumptions, but history and age have me thinking that I'm probably not far from the target on this one. Another consideration is that with six kids, Mrs. Brader just may have her hands full, even if she does have a helper named Alice in the kitchen.

So, it is no big surprise that the Brader kids are parked outside the office while the parents confer with the administrator about their requests. And, if this is a school of any size, this is probably not the first case where home-schoolers are knocking on the door for public education services. I'm sure the administrator has heard the full range of petitions from cooperative to demanding. I remember one time when a parent told me he had saved the district eight years of expenses and now expected some of that money to be used to address his requests for his student as he entered high school. For openers, he wanted all school fees to be waived.

I'm glad I have sound teeth because I might have choked on my dentures when I heard that one.

Brian has done another great job of providing a multitude of possible answers. In fact, Brian has wandered more than usual on this one because the laws regarding homeschool options are so vague and so varied that it is almost impossible to give specific answers for the Brader kids, or for anyone.

To be honest, unless parents just plain enroll their kids on a full-time basis, each case has its own issues to consider, like transportation, available space, course prerequisites, and so on. And Brian didn't even mention things like issues with special education cooperatives considerations, vocational school requirements, and the availability of health-related services. Lastly, we can't forget the fairness factor to other kids. Is it fair for the first seat trombone player to be unseated by the kid that only comes to school an hour a day—maybe just to toot her own horn?

Before I get going on the homeschool kids, let me share two prejudices I have that may taint my perspective on how the Brader family should be treated. First and foremost is my total love for public education. I think that, for the most part, we do a good job educating kids. Unlike factories or other places of employment, we don't have any rejection or selection rights. Whoever walks in the door, lives in the district, and falls within certain very broad age limits is our client. We don't screen them or give them entrance exams. We don't say to them, sorry you don't fit our needs, you are too tall, we have too many in your age bracket, or you are purple and we don't take purple people here. Nope, we take every student, no matter what, and then we educate them, no matter what. Sure, some students will have special needs and get special treatment. Some will be harder to deal with. We won't necessarily like the attitude of some students, or their parent's attitude, or their piercings or multi-colored whatever. But, we will still take them and do our best.

In most circumstances, especially if you let us, in exchange for walking in our doors, we will give each student a ton of skills, much intelligence, loads of common sense, and enough chutzpa to get through life.

We may even teach things like welding, swimming, tap dancing, trigonometry, dressmaking, a foreign language or two, organic chemistry, horticulture, fencing—with swords or boards—and more. Lots more. And we do it with energy, passion, love, and expertise. So here is my dilemma: Why not take advantage of the wonders of public education, where we have labs, gyms, assemblies, sports, orchestras, and accelerated reading programs? Where we put fluoride on teeth and teach driving, how to care, how to read, and how to learn forever? We do it with licensed, certified, professionally trained educators, including teachers, social workers, coaches, and counselors.

Let me assure you that I am not against homeschooling. I understand that for some kids, families, faiths, and situations it works. But honestly, for some it doesn't make sense, and for those, I just have to wonder.

I told you there were two prejudices. The second one is that every kid, no matter what, deserves a fair shake and the best opportunities that these great United States can provide. Thus, when a mom or dad brings a kid to us and asks us to teach them, I feel we must do whatever we can, as fairly as possible, to comply. And this prejudice trumps my concerns about homeschooling. So when the Brader kids come a-knockin' on our door, we need to help them get the best of what we have, the same way we do for every other child in our district.

So, how do we handle the inevitable questions about things like placement, special education, and specific class enrollments? We do it according to Hoyle, which in this case is called Board Policy.

Throughout this book Brian's advice is more specific than general. As I mentioned, in this chapter he wanes from that a bit because it seems that no two states are exactly alike when it comes to how they deal with homeschoolers, and, of course, if you add to the mix the myriad of rules and regulations for special education, it becomes even more confusing. Thus, here is my number one and most rigid recommendation on the homeschool issue: spend the money and the time to have a complete board policy that outlines exactly what your state permits, requires, and allows you to do. If your policy says you accept students at any age and for any reason, but that you must administer specific assessments to determine placement, then your policy should outline exactly what steps are needed. If you have the latitude to make the placement determination, I recommend your policy give specific direction about who, when, where, and what, so that nothing is left to be negotiated or left to politics.

Thus, in returning to our scenario, if Greg wants to enroll in Highland High School, the policy should outline exactly how his past education will or will not be evaluated, what tests he will need to take, and how they will be assessed for grade placement. The policy should also indicate other factors, if applicable, for those entering on a part-time or course-specific basis. The policy should address transportation requirements, textbook and other fees, procedures to determine if a class is available, grading and credit processes, attendance requirements, and how eligibility will be applied.

If there is no policy on point, then the matter should be discussed and agreed upon in a contract or other document between the family and school before the services are being provided. In other words, if possible, leave nothing to chance. Why do all this? Because homeschool situations are anything but normal and routine. Homeschool parents can be very demanding and have unusual expectations—or they can be super cooperative and very easy to work with. Still, leave nothing to chance.

Think through the part-time attendance process fully and make it agreeable and understandable. Enrolling a student in a part-time, course-specific program is tougher than enrolling a student on a full-time basis. Basically, with full-time enrollment, once you determine where a student fits in the program and how past credits and future requirements are measured, it is fairly routine. But when the student wants to be part of the athletic or cocurricular program, or special (advanced, limited, or unique) classes, it can get rather dicey. Do your homework to avoid conflicts and the world will be a much better place for everyone.

Thus, my first and strongest recommendation is to follow the advice of legal counsel, state requirements, the board of education, and state association guidelines. Then, based on those requirements, develop specific, clear, and comprehensive board policies and regulations. Spare no expense having your school attorney review and approve your policies as well.

My second recommendation concerns implementation of these policies. School boards and administrators can be heavy-handed or they can be helpful with the homeschool population. They can take a stance that reflects an attitude that homeschool parents made the decision to avoid the public school systems, so why should the school cater to their needs when they change their minds. On the other hand, educators can do what they should do, which is to help students get the best education possible. Dealing with the homeschool population is indeed an extra level of work and can be a huge, royal pain. However, homeschooling is not going to go away any time soon and we should be in a mindset to handle it the right way, with compassion and professionalism.

Thus, my second recommendation is simple. When homeschool parents come a'knockin' on the old public schoolhouse doors, open them wide, invite them in, and start a'talkin'!

In accommodating homeschool students, first listen to the student's history and the parents' expectations. Set the tone that you care and want to help. Then grab the policy manual, or better yet, have a pullout booklet or document that is reader-friendly, which not only outlines the policies, but also includes a checklist of steps that parents must follow, along with a friendly list of contact names, numbers, and addresses. By doing this, you not only are acting very professional, you are also making it clear that you know what you are doing and how to do it well. Why not make a great first impression when you have the chance?

Go through the document, the check lists, and, if appropriate, other information that you normally share with new families. Make the homeschool student and the parents feel at home, but also let them know that there are specific requirements and expectations involved in their decision to enroll their child in the public school setting.

Principals and counselors may be involved in this process as well as teachers and central office staff. Health exams may be needed. Bus routes may need to be determined. The list goes on. Every situation will be different, so be sure to think through what special circumstances are involved and what personnel might need.

As with every conference, you may want to be sure to think through the "8 Steps to an A+ Conference" as outlined in this book, in order to make this conference productive and life-changing. And don't forget the primary objective when meeting new parents, regardless of whether the parents are new to the community or longtime community members who have homeschooled their children, is to convince them that their school meets (and exceeds) the needs of their children. (And if it doesn't, then ask "why not" and work on ways to fix the problems.)

One final comment. Every child *should* be homeschooled. The home should be a place of learning and wonder, where kids learn and thrive. That brand of homeschooling I'm talking about should support, not replace, the opportunities at the local public school. The local public school will be a place where parents will want their kids to go if it is majestic and not mediocre. That's why we are writing this book, to help everyone, including parents, to do their job as best they can and to make the school and home partners in the learning and teaching process.

Chapter Six

Safeguarding Student Privacy and Records: You Want Me to Stick This Where?

Brian D. Schwartz

Introduction

Family Educational Rights and Privacy Act, widely known as FERPA, applies to all public elementary and secondary schools, colleges, and universities and all private schools that receive federal funding. Additionally, every state has enacted its own student records and privacy laws, most of which are based on and closely follow FERPA. For the purposes of this chapter, we will discuss student records and privacy laws from the federal perspective.

In reading the commentary and case examples that follow, it is important to remember that the law of your particular state may provide for supplemental recordkeeping and privacy requirements. In cases where state law and federal law are different or conflict, it is always advisable to follow the most restrictive requirement. For example, FERPA requires that parents must be given access to their child's education record no later than 45 days after making a request. Illinois law mandates that access be provided within 15 days. In this case, Illinois school districts must follow the more restrictive state law and provide access to parents within 15 days of the request.

Requirements of FERPA

Essentially, FERPA governs the safeguarding, control, and access of education records. Education records (often referred to as "student records") are defined as any documents that (1) contain information directly related to a student and (2) are maintained by the school or entity acting on the school's behalf. Specifically exempted from the definition of education records are teacher or administrator notes that are not generally shared with anyone and records maintained by a law enforcement unit of the school or district. Additionally, effective in late 2008, FERPA regulations were amended to also exempt "peer grading" from the definition of an education record.

This broad definition of education record includes not only records kept in a student's official file but also such things as pictures of students that are maintained by the school, emails that include student names and are maintained on the district's computer server, audiotapes and videotapes maintained by the school, and student grades that are maintained on the district's computer system.

In a nutshell, FERPA requires schools and school districts to safeguard and secure all of these education records. This requires each school to appoint a records custodian—who is usually the principal—to assure that all safeguards are followed. The Act further gives a student's parent or guardian the primary right to access and control the student's education record, with these rights transferring to the student directly when he/she reaches 18 years of age or enters a postsecondary education institution, thereby becoming what FERPA terms an "eligible student."

Specifically, FERPA grants to parents and eligible students four primary rights. Notification of these rights must be made to parents and eligible students on a yearly basis. The actual means of notification (like a special letter, inclusion in a PTA bulletin, student handbook, or newspaper article) is left to the discretion of each school district. Furthermore, school districts are required to effectively notify in their native language parents who have a primary or home language other than English.

The four rights granted by FERPA are as follows:

The right to inspect and review the student's education records maintained by the school. A parent or eligible student must be granted access within a reasonable time, but in no case more than 45 days after making a request. Schools may charge a fee for copies, as discussed below.

The right to request that a school correct record information that is believed to be inaccurate or misleading. If the school determines that the record should not be amended, the parent or eligible student then has the right to a formal hearing. At the hearing, the parents or eligible student must be given a full and fair opportunity to present evidence relevant to the issues raised and may, at their own expense, be assisted or represented by one or more individuals, including an attorney. After the hearing, if the school still decides not to amend the record, the parent or eligible student has the right to place a statement with the record setting forth his or her view about the contested information.

The right to prevent disclosure of the student's education record, subject to several exceptions. This right and the exceptions thereto are discussed more fully below.

The right to complain to FERPA officials if any of the above rights are violated. If a parent or eligible student believes that a school has violated the rights guaranteed by FERPA, a written complaint may be filed with the Family Compliance Office, U.S. Department of Education, 400 Maryland Ave. SW, Washington, DC 20202-4605. The Family Compliance Office investigates each complaint to determine whether the school district has failed to comply with the provisions of FERPA. Complaints must be filed with the Family Compliance Office within 180 days of the date of the alleged violation or the date that the complainant knew or reasonably should have known of the alleged violation. (Note, under FERPA the sole right regarding violations of the Act is to complain to federal officials, as discussed herein. State student privacy laws may, additionally, give parents or eligible students the right to sue for civil damages in state court.)

Of the four rights discussed above, the right to prevent disclosure of a student's education record is perhaps the most widely used and debated. FERPA generally provides that a student's education record and other documents governed by FERPA cannot be released without written permission of the parent or eligible student.

Access to FERPA Records

However, FERPA allows schools to disclose these records, without consent, to the following parties or under the following conditions:

- **To school officials with a legitimate educational interest.** This generally includes school and district administrators, a student's current teachers, other educational professionals working with the student, and coaches of athletic teams on which the student is participating. Schools and school districts must use "reasonable methods" to assure that education records are not released to school officials who do not have a legitimate educational interest in a child.

- **To other schools to which a student is transferring or has transferred.** Here, the student's parents or eligible student must be notified of the transfer, receive a copy of the student record, if desired, and have an opportunity for a hearing to challenge the content of the record.

- **To specified officials for audit or evaluation purposes.**

- **To appropriate parties in connection with financial aid to a student.**

- **To organizations conducting certain studies for or on behalf of the school.**

- **To accrediting organizations.**

- **To comply with a judicial order or lawfully issued subpoena.** (In most cases, the parent or eligible student must also be notified in advance of the disclosure of information made pursuant to a subpoena.)

- **To appropriate officials in cases of health and safety emergencies.** This exception has been interpreted to apply any time that there is a "significant and articulable threat to the health or safety of a student or other individual, considering the totality of the circumstances."

- **To state and local authorities, within a juvenile justice system, pursuant to specific state law.** Here, school officials must review the law of their particular state in determining the extent that their state's law allows for the sharing of information between schools and law enforcement.

- **Pursuant to an established policy on directory information.** Here, schools may disclose, without consent, directory information, which may include a student's name, address, telephone listing, date and place of birth, major field of study, participation in officially recognized activities and sports, weight and height of members of athletic teams, dates of attendance, degrees and awards received, and the most recent school attended by the student. However, schools must tell parents and eligible students exactly what constitutes directory information and allow parents and eligible students a reasonable amount of time to request that the school not disclose directory information.

Limitation on Right to Access Education Record

If the education record of a student contains information concerning another student, the parent or eligible student may not inspect and review that information. Parents only have the right to inspect and review information concerning their children, and eligible students only have the right to inspect and review information concerning them personally. The school or district has the right to redact information that does not directly pertain to the student in question.

Recordkeeping Requirements of the Records Custodian

A school must maintain a record of each request for access to and each disclosure of personally identifiable information from the education records of *each* student. For each request or disclosure of a student's education record, the school must document (1) the party who requested the student record and (2) the legitimate interest the party has in obtaining the information. This recordkeeping requirement is extremely important in the event that there is ever a question concerning whether or not a child's education record was properly accessed. Properly maintained records can go a long way in helping a school district resolve an otherwise expensive and time-consuming legal battle.

Fees to Copy Records

A school district may charge a fee for a copy of an education record which is made for the parent or eligible student, unless the imposition of a fee effectively prevents a parent or eligible student from exercising the right to inspect and review the student's education records. A school district may not, however, charge a fee to search for or to retrieve the education records of a student.

Transfer of Education Records to Third Parties

Personally identifiable information from a student's education record may only be transferred to an authorized third party on the condition that the third party does not permit any other party to have access to such information without the written consent of the parent or eligible student. If a third party permits access to the information in violation of FERPA or fails to destroy the information as required, the school district is prohibited from allowing the third party to access student record information for a period of not less than five years.

Students Who Are 18 and Their Parents

As first discussed above, when a student turns 18 years of age or enters a postsecondary school, he or she becomes an "eligible student" and all rights otherwise accorded to the parents are transferred to the student. Except for limited circumstances—which generally apply to higher education—school officials must communicate directly with eligible students regarding their education records.

However, FERPA does not prevent a school district from giving students who are under the age of 18 certain rights with respect to their education record. For example, school districts may specifically allow students under age 18 to access and view their education record. Likewise, a 2008 interpretation of FERPA by the U.S. Department of Education indicates that parents who claim their child as a dependent for federal income tax purposes may still receive student record information regarding their otherwise eligible child; however, parents are prohibited from making educational decisions regarding their eligible child.

Former Students

FERPA permits school districts to disclose directory information on former students without providing an opt out notice or providing an additional opt out opportunity. FERPA does, however, require schools to honor a former student's opt out request made while the student was in attendance, unless it was specifically rescinded by the former student.

Maintenance of Records by Law Enforcement Agencies

As noted above, records of law enforcement units are specifically exempt from the definition of education record and are therefore not subject to FERPA. According to FERPA regulations, a "law enforcement unit" means any individual, office, or department, including both police officers and security guards that are designated to enforce laws or maintain security and safety within a school or district. A law enforcement unit does not lose its status as such if it also performs other non-law enforcement functions for a school or district, including investigation of incidents or conduct that constitutes or leads to a disciplinary action or proceedings against the student.

FERPA also defines "records of law enforcement unit" as files, documents, and other materials that are created by a law enforcement unit, created for a law enforcement purpose, and maintained by the law enforcement unit. Note, however, documents that otherwise constitute a student record do not lose their status simply because they are transferred to a law enforcement unit. In these cases, the law enforcement unit must safeguard these education records in accordance with FERPA.

Communication by Email

There has been a great deal of debate in the education community as to whether or not the use of emails to communicate with students, their parents, and other faculty violates FERPA. As of the date of this publication, the Family Privacy Compliance Office has yet to issue guidance on this issue. However, suffice it to say that an email can become a student record if the email identifies a student and is maintained on the school district's computer server.

Just because an email creates a student record does not mean that teachers and administrators should refrain from using emails to communicate with parents and with each other. Email provides a wonderful opportunity to open lines of communication and to share information. However, it must be remembered that when sending and receiving emails that contain personally identifiable student information, the aforementioned FERPA rules must be followed!

There are, additionally, a number of other factors that should be considered when communicating by email. First, school districts should assure that their email servers are secure. It is also recommended that school districts require all school staff to use a password prior to logging onto their email account. Also, because email subject lines can often be viewed by individuals other than the sender and receiver of the email—such as the technology coordinator—it is a wise practice not to put any personally identifiable student information in the subject line. This includes a student's name or identification number.

Another important consideration deals with what has popularly been referred to as "spoofing." This is where an illegitimate party attempts to get information by posing as a student's parent or eligible student. School officials should take great care to assure that the individual requesting or being provided with student record information is the parent, eligible student, or other person with a legal reason to have the student record information.

Electronic Gradebooks

Another major concern of the electronic age is the use of computer-based gradebooks and attendance systems. Again, it is important to remember that these tools create student records to the extent that they identify students and are maintained by the school district. School districts should assure that this information is strictly safeguarded and password protected. Only individuals with a legitimate educational interest or other legal need to know should have access to a particular student's record information.

Military Recruiters

Pursuant to the Elementary and Secondary Education Act and No Child Left Behind, school districts that receive federal funds are required to provide certain information to military recruiters. Specifically, secondary schools (grades 9 through 12) must comply with a request by a military recruiter for students' names, addresses, and telephone numbers. However, eligible students or parents who have "opted out" or requested that directory information not be shared are exempt for the reporting requirement.

Additionally, secondary schools must provide military recruiters the same access to students as they generally provide to postsecondary institutions or prospective employers. For example, if the school has a policy of allowing postsecondary institutions or prospective employers to come on school property to provide information to students about educational or professional opportunities, this same access must be extended to military recruiters.

Lastly, as discussed above, federal law requires that parents and eligible students be notified of what material constitutes directory information, which may be disclosed without consent, unless the parent or eligible student opts out. It is further required that the high school include in this notification the fact that the school discloses certain information to the military upon request, subject to the parent or eligible student's ability to opt out.

FERPA and HIPAA

While a full discussion of the Health Insurance Portability and Accountability Act (or HIPAA) is well beyond the scope of this book, a few observations are worth noting. HIPAA was enacted in 1996 to, among other things, improve the privacy of health care information maintained by "covered entities." Covered entities are health care providers that transmit certain health care information in electronic form. Specifically, covered entities must protect an individual's health records and other identifiable health information through specific safeguards and may only release such information with an individual's consent, subject to certain limited exceptions.

As school districts often provide health care services to students and sometimes transmit health care information electronically, it has been questioned whether these schools and school districts are subject to HIPAA. Further complicating the matter have been questions as to whether school districts subject to HIPAA are also subject to FERPA, which provides similar protections with respect to student records. In late 2008—a full twelve years after HIPAA was enacted—the federal government provided some clarification and guidance on these questions.

First, school districts that provide health care to students, through a school nurse, psychologist, or otherwise, are "health care providers" under HIPAA. School districts that provide health care *and* transmit student records electronically in connection with student health care are covered entities and subject to HIPAA. However, even school districts that are covered entities under HIPAA are not usually required to comply with HIPAA's privacy rules because the only health records maintained by the school are education records or treatment records, which are covered by FERPA. Any health records that fall under the protection of FERPA are governed by FERPA and not HIPAA.

Granted, the above alphabet soup of acronyms can be very confusing. If you have just finished reading the above paragraphs multiple times, we guarantee that you are not the only one. Hence, in an attempt to provide clarity, we offer one further attempt to explain from a different perspective.

In order for a school district to be covered under HIPAA, it must provide health care services to students *and* transmit student health care records electronically. Thus, even though a school employs school nurses, physicians, psychologists, or other health care providers, the school is not generally a HIPAA covered entity because the providers do not engage in any of the covered transactions, such as billing a health plan electronically for their services. It is expected that most elementary and secondary schools fall into this category.

Where a school district provides health care to students *and* transmits health care records electronically, such as electronically transmitting health care claims to a health plan for payment, the school is a HIPAA covered entity and must generally comply with the HIPAA. However, even in this case, many schools are exempt from HIPAA requirements because the school maintains health information only in student health records that are education records under FERPA and, thus, not protected health information under HIPAA. Because student health information in education records is protected by FERPA, HIPAA excludes such information from its coverage.

For example, if a public high school employs a health care provider that bills Medicaid electronically for services provided to a student under the IDEA, the school is a HIPAA covered entity and would be subject to the HIPAA requirements. However, if the school's provider maintains health information only in what are education records under FERPA, the school is not required to comply with HIPAA. Rather, the school would have to comply with FERPA's privacy requirements with respect to its education records, including the requirement to obtain parental consent in order to disclose to Medicaid billing information about a service provided to a student.

Case Study #7: Bowling with Hank

Bill and Lucy Dobbs bowl with Marcy and Henry (Hank) Hickman. All four are teachers at Birkley Secondary School. While bowling last week, the main topic of discussion was the recent arrest of a high school junior, Barney "Bubba" Singleton, for the attempted rape of a student from a neighboring school district. Henry mentions that Barney had been suspended from his previous school for similar behavior and spent some time in a juvenile facility before coming to Birkley. Unknown to gabby Hank, one of Bubba's relatives, Uncle Pete, was bowling on the opposing team, and when he heard that, he went into a rage. Pete stated, emphatically, that "no one should know about his nephew's record," and that "hell was going to be paid" for letting Barney's past become public information.

Administrative Perspective:

Brian, before you give us the cold, hard facts about privacy issues and the other legal concerns of this case and possibly suggest that Hank should be brought before a collection of his peers and then be reformatted into a bowling pin, let me talk about some plain old common sense. This case isn't a brain buster, but, unfortunately, I think similar cases probably happen way too often.

First a word to Hank: you are an idiot! Barney's uncle has every right to be madder than get-out with you, and you should probably do exactly that—hope to get out of this situation as soon as possible, with a quick apology to everyone involved and then lots of prayer that you don't end up getting your bowling ball, and other personal property, sued from here to Christmas Island.

I don't know or fully understand the legal ramifications of what Uncle Pete can do to Hank, but Brian has instilled in me the knowledge that anyone can sue for any reason at any time in any place, anyhow. So, unless Hank undoes his stupidity, AFAP (as fast as possible), his rear may be in a ringer. And, quite honestly, it should be.

Still, beyond what appears to be the obvious, which is an inappropriate disclosure of confidential information, it is important to determine how Hank acquired the information in question. Hank may have an out if Barney himself told him of his sordid past. Hank may also have an out if Barney is an adult and his past was printed in the paper. And Hank may have an out if Barney's pre-Birkley history was general knowledge to everyone and, although not verified, a topic of public discussion. Hank may be innocent of disclosing confidential information and just insensitive (and still stupid) for blabbing it in a public place.

No matter what, he can still be in a big pile of legal nuisance if Uncle Pete does indeed plan for "hell to be paid" by old Hank. Hank is already probably lucky that Uncle Pete did not blow a gasket right there in the alley and flatten old Hank with a splitter.

Damage control is needed. A credible and immediate explanation, if there is one, to Uncle Pete, on the spot, might bring this case study to a sudden stop and prevent it from going any farther.

If there is no explanation to be shared, if Hank learned his info from reading Bubba's records, by hearing it in a staff meeting, or from a discussion with a law officer, Hank's in deeper trouble. No matter, a sincere apology never hurts.

If Hank did in fact make a huge blunder with confidentiality, he needs to call his building administrator and report the confrontation ASAP, and he may suggest the building administrator let the superintendent know as well. Surprises of this nature are not well received. Uncle Pete may just be mad enough to call a board member, although he probably won't call the newspaper. On the other hand, after a couple of beers after bowling, he might. One must prepare for the worst.

That's as far as I can go with this. Hank and the school may be contacted by Uncle Pete's lawyer, by Uncle Pete, by the entire Barney-Pete family tree. No one knows for sure. Uncle Pete may also conclude, after a night of bowling, that Barney is only getting what he deserves and may drop the whole thing. No matter what happens or how it is handled, there are a few lessons to be learned from this situation.

First, it is human nature to want to know more than the other guy and come off as a source of juicy information. Educators can't afford to be human at certain times, and this is one of them. Educators must restrain themselves when they are privy to information, confidential or not, that is best avoided. Professional training, adulthood, ethical living, and moral development usually indicate to most educated adults what to say and what not to say, and at what times. It comes with the territory of being a licensed, certified, college-educated educator. Duh.

Second, if you know something you should keep confidential, you have a professional and ethical responsibility to do so. If you can't, you have no business being in our business. Inappropriate sharing of information can permanently damage lives and reputations. This is not a low-calorie topic; this is the real thing.

If you are with other people who know what you know, and you gained the information through appropriate and ethical sources, then by all means discuss it privately, if need be, but *not* at the bowling alley, the grocery store, in the church pew, or at bridge club. It's not a matter of trusting the individuals around you, but an issue of doing what is right.

Finally, even if you learn information outside of school—on the street, in the newspaper, or from your neighbor—don't repeat it if it is potentially dangerous or harmful. When asked, just say, "I really am not sure of the facts, so I better not comment."

Let's hope Uncle Pete rolls a 300 game and forgets about Hank's inappropriate report about Barney.

Legal Perspective:

Unfortunately, Jim, as you know, this situation is all too common. A group of teachers and/or administrators go out one evening and the conversation turns to work. Inevitably, when work is discussed, certain students—and you know who they are—become the main topic of the discussion.

And Jim is right: no good can come from gossiping about students. These conversations, whether they take place at a bowling alley, at dinner, or even over the phone, must stop!

From a legal perspective, the obvious question concerns whether Hank violated state or federal student privacy laws in disclosing Barney's criminal record. The most important element is *how* Hank became aware of Barney's past in addressing this question. If Hank obtained this information though Barney's education record or through his position as a teacher at the school, FERPA—the federal student records act —may be implicated.

As you will recall, FERPA essentially provides that student education records and education record information cannot be disclosed except with permission of a student's parent or guardian. There are several exceptions to this rule, but none of them apply to this situation, where Hank is obviously not acting in Barney's best interest. Hank might try to argue that he was sharing the information for educational and student safety purposes, but given the situation and venue, I think this is a stretch.

If Hank did indeed violate FERPA, Barney's parent or guardian (or Barney himself if he is 18 years of age or older) has the right to file a complaint with the U.S. Department of Education's Family Compliance Office. If the complaint is found to be valid, the school district could be sanctioned, which ultimately could include the withholding of certain federal funds. According to a recent U.S. Supreme Court case, *Gonzaga University v. Doe*, there is, however, no private cause of action under FERPA. This simply means that parents and eligible students cannot sue a school district directly for violations of FERPA. The only remedy under FERPA is to complain to federal officials.

Parents and eligible students can, however, generally sue a school district directly for violations of state privacy laws. These lawsuits can—and have—resulted in significant monetary awards. Additionally, parents and eligible students have successfully brought lawsuits against school districts based on tort theories, such as defamation of character and intentional infliction of emotional distress. These lawsuits can be pursued even if the information that is disclosed does not meet the definition of an education record.

In addition to the potential liability to the school district, Hank might find himself in significant hot water. First, the school may be able to discipline Hank for his actions, and depending on a variety of factors, his career may be in peril. Also, the school district may refuse to indemnify Hank in any lawsuit brought against Hank as a teacher, as he clearly stepped outside the course and scope of his duties and failed to act reasonably. Lastly, Barney and his family may be able to institute a civil lawsuit against Hank personally for damages to Barney's character and reputation. In this case, the three strikes against Hank are not a good thing. If it were baseball instead of bowling, Hank would indeed be out!

“For every complex problem, there is a solution that is simple, neat, and wrong.”

H.L. Mencken

Chapter Seven

Teacher, Administrator, and Board Member Speech: Bite Your Tongue!

Jim Burgett

Introduction

Wouldn't it be nice if there were a clear and concise set of rules for who did what, where, and when? Actually, it *wouldn't* be nice because it would stifle creativity, spontaneity, and passion. One thing we know about education is that every day is a new day and every issue is truly an opportunity. Thus, there are no "rules" governing the interaction between the players. There are some guidelines, and I guess Robert does have a set of Rules about how to play fair during meetings, but the rest, well, the rest is left up to us—to decide, conquer, and facilitate.

What I hope to share in this very broad chapter on speech and behavior are some general guidelines that might help both the paid and the unpaid who rule our schools. In one way or another, these musings should help keep the process civil, even though, for the most part, they are not civil law. They are good, clean, common sense thoughts that, if considered and implemented, might just help us work together as we try to accomplish our number one goal: providing the best education for kids using the resources available. Also, by properly communicating with each other, maybe it will be easier to find Middle Ground.

So let me give you a handful of general guidelines that just might be helpful at school, at home, and in life.

The **first guideline** goes all the way back to pre-K. Say please and thank you. One of the basic rules of good governing is to be nice. It also applies to good leadership, good communication, and just about everything else that follows the word good. Being nice does not mean you must agree or that you have to shelve your opinions next to your hat and gloves. What it does mean is that when you talk, you do it nicely. When I was in grade school, I heard a lot of cuss words. When I was in fifth grade, I used them, but I had enough sense not to use them in the classroom or around most adults. And, since I liked my head attached to the rest of my body, I never cussed around my mother. Sadly, my father would have feigned anger, but probably would have also sighed in relief that I was becoming a "man." What I also learned in those early years is that swearing and rudeness had a way of making people angry and starting fights. Unfortunately, I witnessed it firsthand too often at home. Being nice paid dividends. Being rude and using inappropriate language caused division.

Over my decades of school employment, I have watched some masterful communicators discuss difficult topics in ways that melted opposing sides of an argument, flattened anger and mistrust, and made enemies act decently with each other. It was a skill I have always wanted to master, and I've worked hard to refine over the years. Call it mediation, call it communication leadership, call it anything you want, but it is basically the art of remaining calm, collected, and polite. It is a balance of listening to others, repeating what they say, developing consensus, and negotiating a truce, agreement, or solution. It is fundamental to developing trust and building relationships.

Let's talk about board members. Board members are often lay people with little familiarity with setting policy for a school district. They typically have little experience with education in general, other than having once been a student. Board members are entrusted with tons of money, grandiose facilities, and the future of the world. What an assignment—and usually with no pay!

Many have their own opinions, often based on good or bad experiences, their own kids, or things they hear from the neighbors or friends on the golf course, at the bowling alley, or at card club. They mean well and they are willing to give their time and energy to make the school a better place. That's exacerbated by the fact that some of them simply don't understand the importance of being a good listener or communicator.

Fortunately, it's a very small percentage, but when it happens, when a board member flies off the handle or goes nuts for a minute or two—or a month or a term—it can be a disaster. This is when their teammates, the other board members, need to jump in and help bring the conversation back to the land of productivity. Board members who work together can make a huge difference, and by working as a team, they can compensate for strengths and weaknesses of individual members.

Parents can also present a communication challenge, and how we handle them usually determines both our individual and corporate sanity and success.

Let me share a true experience I had with a mom. I'll call her Mrs. F—and she liked to drink. She usually kicked it into high gear about noon and was blasted by 2 or 3 in the afternoon, just about the time she liked to make her first call to complain about a teacher, principal, or coach that had mishandled one of her too numerous children. Alas, she called me! Sometimes she called because one of her kids complained that the lunch was too cold the day before, or too hot, or the fries were baked instead of fried. The topic of the day was always a mystery, but usually trite in the scope of life's major challenges.

I call her Mrs. F. because that is a hint to her favorite word. As a new superintendent, I initially took her calls and tried to work through her rudeness and inappropriate comments. I was always polite and patient. About the fifth time she called me, she told me (she didn't ask) to take a trip south. To be more exact, she told me to go to hell. I told her, very politely, that I did not use the kind of language she uses, that I would never tell her to go to hell, and that I did not, and would not, engage in any discussion, now or in the future, that wasn't civil and polite. I warned her that I was going to hang up, and if she wanted to speak with me, she would have to stay on the topic, be polite, and not swear. If she couldn't do that, then we couldn't talk. I politely hung up. I assumed she would call back immediately, and I told my secretary I would get it. She did, and she called me a name that is similar to a rear-end human exhaust orifice, and once again told me where to go and hung up. She must have felt proud to get in the last word. Later than night, many drinks later that night, she called me at home, hardly intelligible. After a few words, I told her not to call me when she had been drinking, to respect the fact that I was polite to her, and she should return the courtesy. I told her not to call back, and if she did, I would not answer. She did. I didn't. She stopped trying. She had probably passed out.

Mrs. F called me the very next morning. She was sober. She told me I was a prude and that I probably knew how to swear like a sailor, but she would try to comply with my wishes. She only used the "F" word twice, but apologized with a snide remark. We talked and from that moment on made progress. All it took was being firm, polite, calm, and fair. It takes patience and prudence to communicate with some people, but by remaining polite and determined, you often gain their respect. By the way, I directed my office to never accept a call from her after noon, and oddly enough, within a few weeks, all her calls came during her sober hours. She was actually sort of nice when she was sober, and we did work through a number of issues, which eventually reduced her calls to almost zero. She went from a school enemy to a school advocate.

I have one more example to share, and it too is real. Two administrators work in the same office. Let's name them Bob and Ray. Both share the same team of administrative assistants, secretaries, or clerical aides—whatever you decide to title them. Bob is bossy and borderline rude. He doesn't give or expect any more work from the ladies in the office than does Ray, but he seldom asks and even less often says thanks. He is a bit demanding and hasty. A nice guy, liked by the kids and teachers, a longtime veteran who will have the job until he falls over or retires, but Bob thinks that the office is there to serve him. Period.

Now Ray has similar characteristics, is equally liked by students and staff, has job security, and is just as productive as Bob. One difference separates Bob and Ray, and it is not a comedic routine. Ray is polite and appreciative of everyone all the time. He never demands and always asks. He never forgets to say thank you, even leaves a note on a desk once in while when a project or request is done above and beyond.

The office ladies love him. How do I know this? I gave a workshop on school quality once and afterwards had the opportunity to sit down with a group of administrative assistants who worked for both Bob and Ray. Just by his being kind and polite, they were willing to do anything for Ray. Bob's work demands were similar to Ray's, but while they would do anything for Ray, they would only do the minimum for Bob. It all had to do with please, thank you, appreciation, and being nice.

The **second guideline** is a bit harder to master, but it is simple as well. Don't always assume that your way is the only way, or that you are always right. Trust me, there have been many times when I regretted not taking a few courses in podiatry, to help me remove my foot from my own mouth. It took me a while (well, years) to realize that even I, the multi-degreed, multi-certified leader of the free world (at least of the school district) didn't have all the answers and that this woman or that man who worked on a farm, or in a store, or was a dental assistant, often knew more than I did. When I finally learned that, it switched from being a game of who had all the answers to a collaboration of finding the best answers. Life suddenly got a lot easier—and more productive.

So my second guideline is simply to respect the contributions of those who communicate with you. To do this, it means that you have to master a difficult skill: keeping quiet. You have to master the art of listening, which requires more than just looking at someone with your ears unplugged. It means looking at them, processing what they say, trying to "be" who and where they are, and being open to their input. Not easy in many cases, but essential for productive communications. I have also learned that restating and reconfirming are important steps in processing.

Case in point: Mrs. Geldhart comes in to complain that her daughter Sally is struggling with her eighth grade teacher, Mr. Leonard. It seems Sally just can't pass a test in his class. The complaint is that Mr. Leonard is too tough, inconsistent, and gives too much homework. Sally is getting a "D" for the first time in her life, and her mother wants her transferred to another class. You listen quietly, encourage Mrs. Geldhart to tell her story, don't interrupt her, and take mental notes of things you want clarified. After she finishes, you "restate" her story so that the main points, as you heard them, are highlighted. You then ask her specific questions about what you have successfully restated, things like: she fails all tests (but is earning a D), the teacher is not consistent (and yet she indicates the teacher gives regular homework, quizzes, and tests), and he is too tough (yet she was sent a progress report, an offer for assistance with Sally's work, and there is no indication that Sally is negligent in her efforts). Finally, that she wants Sally transferred from Mr. Leonard to another teacher.

You listened, you restated, you clarified. Now you can communicate. The process lets you make lemonade from lemons. It doesn't take long to understand that Mrs. Geldhart is frustrated about Sally's progress, and you know that Mr. Leonard is one of your best teachers—kind, compassionate, and willing to go the extra mile with kids and families. You now ask a few questions, like, "What did Mr. Leonard say when you talked to him about Sally?" And you are not surprised when you discover that all communications have been by email or note. You ask if either Mrs. or Mr. Geldhart is able to offer Sally any help. They say no because neither of them understand algebra. You ask if Sally has any assistance from a tutor or friend, and you find out that Sally is a cheerleader, works at the convenience store, dates Billy Bob, and has a full work and social calendar. Make time for a tutor? Are you kidding?

You listened, you restated, you asked some necessary questions, and you set up a solution—a meeting with Mrs. Geldhart and Mr. Leonard and help from a student in the student assistance pool during Sally's study hall Mrs. Geldhart was satisfied, and Sally was closer to unraveling the mysteries of algebra! What did all that take? A little time, some patience, listening skills, and some problem solving. And in the process, you found out that Mrs. Geldhart had something to offer, something of value to build upon. Maybe from listening to her you are able to talk to your staff about initiating a *phone call* to the parents of students who might need tutorial assistance instead of the usual progress report and mandatory email. From hearing, came learning and change.

Number three might be the most violated guideline of all. It is simply to join the team. This business of education truly is a huge team effort. And guess who is on the team? Just about everyone. And there are far too many folks who think it a competition between elements within the system. There are far too many situations of "us versus them." "Us" could be the teachers and "them" could be the administration. "Us" could be the board and "them" the association (or unions if that is your mindset). "Us" could be the taxpayers and "them" could be the tax-setters (board). "Us" could be the administration and "them" could be the parents, like when decreased revenue initiates a reduction in programs. "Us" could be the school district and "them" could be the feds, like when we don't get the funding to implement a new program, like *No Child Left Behind.*

"Us versus them" may be the oldest game in the world, but it doesn't make for a productive school system that is focused on doing what is best for kids. And don't forget that "us" could be the evaluator and "them" could be the teacher when the ability to communicate common goals and ways to achieve them is lost in the process. So how do you defeat the "us versus them" mentality and malady?

The process is not that hard, but realizing the talent to get it done can be tricky. The most important step is to truly realize that we are, indeed, all on the same team, with the same goal, moving down the field in the same direction. We can disagree along the way, but we still need to move toward the same goal post.

Teachers and boards can debate the amount of pay increase, but that does not mean they have to come to odds, halt progress, call each other names, paint signs, and walk around in circles refusing to work. Coming to an impasse means defeat. It means you can't compromise or move together. It means you have joined two teams and are now fighting each other. Each time this happens, the system is branded, wounded, and scarred. Progress is slowed down or stopped. Feelings are hurt, divisions are etched, and goals are confused.

Recently, a very serious tragedy happened in a church near my home. A deranged young man walked in and shot and killed the minister during a Sunday service. He also injured two parishioners who tried to help. That church is forever branded. Those who drive by will, for a long, long time, say, "that is the church where the minister was killed." It's a growing church with a progressive, beautiful group of believers in a fantastic facility, but all of that will take a back seat to their unfortunate label of "where the minister was murdered."

I know a district where they had a wayward principal who was caught tampering with some state achievement tests. It was reported in the papers throughout the state, and the principal was sentenced to forty years of correcting bad English themes, or some such punishment. But, no matter, that school is now known as the school that cheated on their state tests. That is sad because it is a good district with dedicated teachers, a caring community, and neat kids.

When a player on the education team won't be a team member, play by rules that are fair and reasonable, debate rather than argue, compromise rather than confuse, talk rather than scream, he risks "branding" the system as cantankerous, negative, anti-kids, strike happy, or worse.

And when a person joins a board with a vendetta or a single-issue purpose, with no intention of listening or learning, that person immediately puts that system at risk of either failure or delayed success. If you join the team, play like a team. It doesn't have to be 7-0 in favor of everything, but it does have to be a team that represents an honest, fair attempt to learn the facts and make a collaborative decision through compromise and honest effort.

What am I saying? Am I saying that there should never be a strike? That a board member should never stand alone on principle and refuse to compromise his or her beliefs? That a parent has no right to lose his or her temper when he or she senses or experiences injustice? Am I saying that teachers don't have the option to argue an unfair directive? Or that educators have all the answers and are thus excluded from listening to public opinion? I'm ***not*** saying any of those things. I am saying that ***it is possible*** to avoid strikes, discuss and solve conflicts, ask and consider explanations, seek rightful answers in a peaceful and productive manner, and, in general, be nice, communicate with an open mind, and stay on the same team.

If we in education can't lead the way in conflict management and problem solving, then how can we teach the world to do the same? If we can't listen and talk, outline and debate, discuss and compromise, then really who can? If we can't walk the talk we teach, then maybe we shouldn't be on the team to begin with.

If you think, from my comments, that I am intolerant of intolerance, you are half right. If you replace the word intolerant with impatient, you are totally right. I am very impatient when I confront intolerance because it is not productive in moving forward, and in this profession we can't stand still or we will be run over by the world.

So, this chapter is rather void of specific "laws" from Brian's books of statutes and dictates. It is, however, filled with common sense and helpful guidelines. I have outlined only three, but they are major.

- Be nice.
- Respect all players and their contributions.
- Be part of the team.

Master these three guidelines as you focus on the goal of education, which is to provide the best education possible within the resources available, and you will accomplish wonders. Guaranteed.

Post Script: If you are working in a school district where communications lack effectiveness, where trust is limited, where teachers don't get along with administration, where board members think they rule the world and prefer micromanaging policy development, or where progress takes a back seat to pettiness, then step up to the plate and start a discussion. Talk to someone, anyone, who you think can start an effective effort to initiate change. Change starts with one person doing one thing. Be that person. I'd also suggest that you go to the bookstore and grab any book written by John Maxwell, the guru of communication and leadership and share what you learn. This business of education is too important, too fundamental to the success of the world, to be left to chance. One person can make a difference. You can be that person.

Case Study #8:
In the Closet

Mrs. Green, the third grade teacher, and Mr. Moore, the custodian, were caught in the janitor's closet at 4:50 p.m. Mrs. Shoemaker went into the closet to return a broom that her students had used and came upon the pair in a heated embrace. Mrs. Green's blouse was open and Mr. Moore's belt was loose. Mrs. Shoemaker said nothing to either party but immediately called the principal as soon as she got home. Mrs. Shoemaker also failed to answer several calls that night from Gary Green (Mrs. Green's husband) and Mr. Moore.

Administrative Perspective:

I hate this case study. Why? I hate it because it happens too often.

Ask a group of veteran administrators how many of them have had to deal with an "in-house" relationship that they thought could be classified as "inappropriate," and I'm going to tell you that many more hands will go up than you might suspect.

Ask a supervisor at a factory the same thing, and I imagine you will see just as many hands. Ask someone at an office how many "office relationships" they have witnessed, and again, it will seem like the norm rather than a rarity. Why?

Maybe it has to do with hormones, or sexuality, or unhappy marriages, or proximity, or cleavage, or SpongeBob Square Pants. Who knows? But we all do know one thing—it happens, and probably always will.

So what do we do about it? Let me share some of my personal thoughts, some from experiences, some shared by others.

The first thing is to be sure you know what you think you know. If you walk into a dark closet and two people are inside with their clothes ruffled and their faces red and nothing coming from their vocal chords, chances are they weren't in there doing research on carbon footprints. But, you *really don't know* unless they were in a mad (or even semi-happy) embrace, sexually involved, or demonstrating some activity that left nothing to your imagination. If they were just there, even with their clothing off kilter a bit, and you didn't see anything happening, then in fact you didn't see anything happen. They know they were caught and you know they were caught and they suspect you won't forget it. They might concoct the most amazing excuse or situational suggestion, but you know that they know that you know.

So, be sure you have the facts. In this case study, we assume that the shocked Mrs. Shoemaker, who is probably still shaking, tells the principal the facts and just the facts. Let's assume she said something like this, "At 4:50 this afternoon, I went to the closet to return a broom. I discovered Mrs. Green and Mr. Moore in the closet, and they scared the beegeebees out of me. I didn't say anything, but noticed Mrs. Green's blouse was askew and Mr. Moore's belt was partially open. They were facing each other, and their eyes popped open wide when the lights came on. They were doing nothing as a unit, but moving quickly individually. That's the end of the story."

The ball has been dropped plunk in the principal's lap.

Later that night Mrs. Shoemaker notices on her caller ID several phone calls from the residences of Mrs. Green and Mr. Moore. She wisely decides to let the prerecorded voice take the messages. It turns out that Mr. Green, not Mrs. Green is calling, as well as Mr. Moore. I wonder, could it be that Mrs. Green told her husband about the closet caper? And are the phone calls being made to find out what Mrs. Shoemaker is going to do with her information? Needless to say, Mrs. Shoemaker has a rougher time catching some winks that night than she did catching her workmates in the closet.

Kudos to Mrs. Shoemaker for reporting what she saw. The behavior she witnessed was inappropriate for a number of reasons. What if a student was sent to the closet with the broom? What if the first grade teacher, who is near retirement and has a bum ticker, had discovered the pair lurking in the closet? What if, what if... And just what is the matter with two school employees when they jump into a closet during working hours for a quick playtime? Yes, Mrs. Shoemaker, you did the right thing both in reporting the discovery and then not answering your phone. Now the matter is off your plate, but I still would hope you would take the time to document everything you saw, the times, the circumstances, the details, and exactly what you reported to the principal, plus the information from your answering machine—names, times, and messages. Why? You might need to remember the details if this incident gets messier than it already is.

The broom, so to speak, is now in the principal's closet. What she does with it is very important. She can't very well ignore the situation since it was reported to her by a staff member. She can't pretend it isn't important since the very incident reeks of inappropriateness. She just has to do something and do it soon.

Here's what I suggest. First, call the superintendent and, together, call the district's lawyer. Spell it out to him or her and get some direction as to how to proceed. I imagine the lawyer will ask some questions before rendering a suggestion. Have either Green or Moore caused problems for you in the past? Is the work performance of Green or Moore satisfactory, or do you see some concerns? Is there anything noteworthy about the work record of any of the employees involved? Is there anything unusual concerning either of their personal lives or their relationship at school? Assuming the answers do not bring to light any existing issues, then I assume that the lawyer would advise you about what you don't know and should be wary of. You don't know anything about what they were doing. You can't discipline them for being in a closet, since closet standing is probably not prohibited by any of your 1,432 board policies. You can't discuss the Green/Moore relationship if it isn't affecting their work performance, but you can discuss the fact that the Green/Moore closet discovery did result in a work-related issue when it frightened or concerned a fellow teacher.

It is my thought that by simply calling the two into the office and sharing that Mrs. Shoemaker reported the event, was startled and concerned by it, and was glad that she returned the broom rather than sending one of the students that stayed after school might be enough warning and enlightenment to jar the Green-Moore dynamic into a more appropriate mindset.

If it were me, I would end the discussion with an opportunity for either or both of them to comment on the event, allowing them to either apologize, beg forgiveness, and repent for their total stupidity or to offer some bizarre excuse that only humans can devise. No matter what they say, you have told them three things: (1) I know, (2) Mrs. Shoemaker knows, and (3) you both know that we know. If they truly have at least half a brain between the two of them, *and there are no other issues to consider*, this case should be closed.

I would follow up with a call or conference with Mrs. Shoemaker. I would thank her profusely for sharing her concern and let her know that you have taken appropriate action with Green and Moore. I would also thank her for submitting a written report on the incident and say that it would be prudent to avoid discussing the details, and if she is asked questions by either party, their relations, or anyone else, that she can say that I have asked that all questions be directed to me.

In most cases this should end the issue and end it for good. If, however, Green or Moore isn't bright enough to behave or in some way makes problems for Shoemaker, then I would enlist the attorney to outline the next steps, which very well could include disciplinary action.

Legal Perspective:

I hate this scenario, too. Jim is certainly correct in that this type of thing happens more than we care to admit, but I hate it for another reason. Dealing with inappropriate relationship issues at school takes a great deal of time and energy and can get extremely messy, especially if there are spouses and families involved. And, as more than one administrator has said to me, "I really didn't think that *this* kind of thing was part of the job…"

Jim gives great advice on dealing with the issue from a practical standpoint. As Jim also properly points out, this is a difficult case to deal with from a teacher discipline / legal perspective. In most jurisdictions, teachers can be disciplined for bad teaching and for bad conduct, and this situation definitely falls within the latter category. However, the exact disciplinary scheme is very much subject to state law and local practices. Therefore, let me make a couple of general comments.

I feel comfortable in saying that in most jurisdictions a teacher can be disciplined for engaging in this type of inappropriate conduct on school property. This, however, is probably not an offence that could lead to an employee's termination, unless the employee was previously warned and this is a pattern of misconduct.

Disciplinary implications and/or notices to remedy conduct should be tied to violations of school district policy or state or local law. Any discipline based on "immorality" is constitutionally suspect.

Even if the school district's administration elects not to discipline the employees, this situation needs to be documented. Documentation needs to include a warning given to the employee not to engage in this type of conduct in the future.

If the employee is in a union, the employee has a right for a union representative to be present during any interview that the employee reasonably believes may result in disciplinary consequences. Employers who fail to allow union representation in these cases and continue with an interview of the employee potentially commit an unfair labor practice.

This goes without saying, but I am going to say it anyway: Taking disciplinary action against a female teacher but not a male teacher or against a married teacher but not against an unmarried teacher could result in charges of discrimination under federal law.

Case Study #9:
1% or 10%—The Game Begins

Haley Lynch meets with the superintendent. It's January and time to set up the first of the estimated dozen meetings between the Green Acres Teacher Association and the Green Acres Board of Education (GATA versus GABE) as they venture to settle a new teacher's contract. History dictates the process, and Haley comes with no other agenda then getting the first date locked in—but she encounters an unexpected response from the superintendent, who tells Haley that she would like to talk to her about the proposal and the expectation of the process.

"What?" asks Haley. "You want to discuss negotiations before we even begin the series of meetings?" The superintendent smiles and nods yes.

Before Haley can mouth "Let me get back to you on that," she hears herself saying, "Why not?"

The superintendent says "Great!" and sets up a meeting between the two for the day after next, right after school. Thus begins a change in procedure, and maybe a change in climate.

Administrative Perspective:

The game of negotiations is often just that, a game. It starts with one side asking for the moon and the other side offering an insult. One meeting follows the next, and the only thing accomplished, besides closing the salary gap from a smaller moon shot to a lesser insult, is the agreement on some "throwaway" language issues. It all amounts to a lot of nonsense and many times opens up opportunities for miscommunication, lack of communication, or a waste of communication. I remember, with great clarity, a discussion where I was told there would be at least eight more meetings conducted between the board and teachers before any settlement because they were four percent apart in salary and they only moved one half percent per meeting. Total craziness.

And then there are the "throwaway" discussion points, items brought up that they won't agree upon—a fact known before the negotiations begin. Sometimes the issues themselves aren't reasonable or rational. They are part of the process just so one side can appear to be willing to concede certain issues, thus truly negotiating in good faith by being able to give as well as take. More nonsense, and both sides usually know it.

You might think I am against negotiations, and you would be right, but only the silly kind. I am also smart enough to know that the "right" or "need" to negotiate does exist in this less than perfect world, and we must be savvy to the process, rules, and guidelines, but not be held hostage to the insanity of negotiating for the sake of negotiating. I am also aware of many districts that only need to conduct one or two negotiation sessions before they finalize a contract that has been discussed for months, or years, through a reasonable and professional ongoing process. I love this type of negotiations.

One time a representative for a teachers' association (not union) told me that negotiations were absolutely necessary for the membership to feel they were getting something for their dues. In other words, the association had to show some "work" to earn the $600 the members paid each year. If they were able to get a decent contract without negotiations, the members might wonder why they were paying the dues? (By the way, unions, in my mind, represent hourly wage earners. Associations represent professional wage earners.) Of course, if communications between the association and the administration were ongoing and regular and allowed for a smooth and streamlined negotiation process, the membership would see that their leaders were working all year for the same positive results, rather than digging in for a few months with several lengthy meetings.

So when the superintendent says to Haley "Let's talk before we negotiate," it is a good start. But, the best start, in my opinion, is to start talking soon after the prior contract is negotiated, finalized, and implemented. Why not start during the first month of school after a new contract is in place? A team of administrators (business, curriculum, super, for example) might meet with a team from the association (president, vice president, and a past or possible negotiator). This informal meeting is not a negotiation session. It is a discussion of issues and items that either team can bring forward and talk about. It is an ongoing listing of concerns or a sharing of successes. It is a time to discuss a possible stipend for teachers who earn National Board Certification or maybe language that allows new teachers two days a year to observe their mentors. Or possibly talk about the change in tenure laws proposed by the state and how that might impact the current evaluation process.

Maybe hold a discussion about the rumblings going on concerning a new principal or the concerns from parents about the way teachers are absent at parent-teacher conferences. These are good old-fashioned, sit-down discussions from both sides of the aisle that can result in substantial changes along the way. Unfortunately, in many schools, problems are stored up for negotiations and then are blasted away at the opposing side like a "blindside" on *Survivor.* Ongoing talks are also excellent opportunities for the administration to share finances with the association as a continuing process, not a shockwave of desperation and smoke and mirrors. This develops not only an educated understanding of operations, but also ownership. A simple communication that states, "Here is the budget, here are the expected revenues, and here is what we are facing."

So when it comes to a discussion between Haley and the superintendent, I'm all for it. I would love for them to sit down, agree upon a team of folks (like I mentioned above) to meet regularly to deal with issues as they happen, might happen, or to keep them from happening.

There is a word I have been using that I just don't like. The word is "sides," as in administration/board versus teachers/staff. Yuck. The only sides that I think truly exist are these: (1) those who want kids to get a good education and (2) those who don't care about education. Now that is a battle I would love for us to suit up for, but associations vs. boards? Never. If we aren't on the same side, shooting for the same principles, running toward the same end zone, then we are so far off base we shouldn't be in the profession. We can work together to solve differences of opinions, but we should never take sides—that indicates battle, and we shouldn't be battling for the same result. Too many districts talk about the teachers association as evil, or the board of education as narrow minded, or the administration as Hitler-like. When these descriptors (or similar substitutes) are used, there is a problem with one of the fundamental spokes of the wheel of success: teamwork. You can't have teamwork if there isn't a team. You can divide up a team by task, by title, or by function, but if the goal is mutually understood and desired, it's achieved through teamwork, not by fighting each other for individual victories.

Is there a legal issue here? I don't think so unless some school law (board policy, signed contract, state labor law) specifically says you can't sit down and talk about mutual concerns that might provide a good working place and/or support for fulfilling the mission of the school. There may be some limiting language that says you cannot agree to a salary increase outside of approved negotiations, but you wouldn't do that in an informal session anyway. What you might do informally is teach the teachers about budgets, income, and available cash, and you might learn, informally, what the teachers feel is a fair compensation in the economic climate of the day. Discussions, if handled correctly for the right reasons and with an understood desire for improvement and understanding, can change the climate of an institution for the better almost immediately, all through legal and appropriate avenues of positive and productive communication.

I think Brian would be the first to contend that honest communications are key to the success of almost anything—running a business, marriage, achieving goals, running a school, and just about everything else on the plate called life.

So how do we do it? How do we get from conflict to concert, from fighting to friends, from hatred to handshakes? The process might take a long time, or it might move along quickly. No matter how long it takes, it must be based on three fundamentals: trust, persistence, and desire. Parties must trust the participants and the motive. Persistence is imperative because there is likely to be some stumbling along the way. Desire to make things better, to streamline the process, work on problems, or join hands in meeting the mission—whatever the stated goals. "We want this to work" has to be the mutual mantra of everyone involved. So, once you understand what it takes, the first step is to find a Haley or a superintendent with the courage to initiate the process and a counterpart with the heart and fortitude to board the train.

Let me end this case study with some questions about communications in your school or district. Do problems fester until they explode? Do people hold back their opinions, afraid to speak out? Do the teachers or the administrators perpetuate the "us vs. them" illness? Is there a lack of ongoing, honest, sincere, and productive communications between members of the team of educators? Instead of one big team fighting for the kids, can you name several teams (custodians, teachers, board of education, bus drivers, disgruntled parents, etc.), each with its own agenda? If you answered yes to any of these questions, then think about this last one: what are you doing to get things on the right track? All it takes is just one person to start the discussion. Just one.

Legal Perspective:

Like Jim, I advocate open communication. In fact, that is the entire purpose of this book, the search for Middle Ground. In particular, bargaining a contract can be a nasty process that may indeed produce a contract, but may also result in damaged relationships that may never be repaired. Frequently, both sides seek to get the community involved in the negotiations as they advocate for their cause, and often it is the students who get caught in the crossfire. So anything that can be done to assist with civil, rational communication can only be viewed as a positive.

The above being said, I must throw in a qualified "however." (After all, that is what lawyers do!) Both sides to the negotiations process must be very careful to follow all state laws governing labor relations. One such law that almost universally applies where there is an employee union is that negotiations must be done collectively and conducted through the bargaining unit's official representatives. Hence, conversations between Haley and the superintendent are okay and can even be productive, but may not cross the line where actual negotiations are being conducted on behalf of the union and management.

That being said, I don't have much additional advice to offer. I have somewhat mixed feelings about lawyers being involved on either side of the bargaining table. Sometimes lawyers are effective in that they can help keep negotiations moving and assure that laws and processes are followed. Additionally, lawyers can be the "bad guys," serve as the scapegoats, and then be cast into the desert when the negotiations are complete. I have also seen cases where lawyers only serve to exacerbate the differences and add to the tension and angst of the process. Hence, in deciding to involve legal counsel at the bargaining table, it is important to pick your representative carefully, then clearly state the lawyer's role in the process.

Chapter Eight

Dealing with Divorce, Difficult Parents, and Other Family Issues: "A-Parent" Authority

Jim Burgett

Introduction

Some chapters in this book do not fall under a single legal category. This is one of them. When we deal with families, parents, parent types, or parent wannabes, the issues fall under many headings. Those include privacy and records, constitutional rights, homeschool issues, custody or court directives, or notification rights. One thing is for sure; the variety of issues seems limitless and the effect of family situations on students is serious business.

This is a chapter that deals more with trust and tact than with policy and procedure. While it is imperative that educators understand their responsibilities and restrictions, it is also imperative that educators do not forget two fundamental overriding philosophies of why we exist. First and foremost, we are here to provide the best education possible to our students, within the resources available. The second fundamental responsibility, which falls primarily under the auspices of administration, is to provide the best staff possible. Implementing these two goals will almost guarantee a successful school system that meets the needs of kids.

Can we talk a minute about our concept of the family? According to United States Census information, and supported by numerous studies, the traditional family concept (two biological parents and their kids) is on the increase. Although it was the norm in the time of our great grandparents, it dropped to about 50% in the late 1960's, then down to 36% by the late 1990's. In 2008, it is back up to around 45%. Overall, about 7 out of 10 kids today live with both biological parents, and of those sets of parents, about 70% are married.

Frankly, I have no idea what the above statistics mean, other than if our kids are better off living with two biological parents, more of them are better off right now.

From my personal experience, I can tell you that for the first 13 years of my life I lived in a traditional family setting, and then for the rest of my life, my family was as non-traditional as could be, and neither situation was ideal. In fact, the traditional environment was far more rocky, relationship wise, than what followed.

I also know that, once, when I was a principal, a family came to register their kids in the middle of the school year. There were five kids, two parents, and between them they had seven different last names. The parents were not married. When they showed up, I thought, "Oh, no, this is going to be trouble." They were low-income, mixed race, and two of the kids needed special education services. The parents appeared to be undereducated, whatever that means, and we immediately typecast the whole unit in the "problem" category. However, I don't recall ever having met two parents who supported the school and their kids more than those folks did. The kids were clean and polite and worked hard. The parents were limited in some skills, but not in love and devotion.

When they moved the next year, we felt a sincere sense of loss. While on every chart they were defined "non-traditional," they had all the attributes most families strive for, just without the materialistic wealth.

When you deal with parents, you simply deal with people, not statistics. Every kid, every mom, every dad, every sibling has a need. Our job is not to judge the relationship choices of the parents, or adults, but to be a protector of the rights of the children and to provide the best care and most love possible during the times we are standing *in loco parentis*, or in place of the parent.

Our job starts when the family first enrolls or when parameters change. We need to have a well-defined procedure for gathering information when parents first enroll their kids in school. We have a right and obligation to understand the structure of the family, within certain restrictions, and to ask questions about the legal and social structure of the unit. We need to know if the parents have custodial rights, visitation rights, live in the same household, and if there are special restrictions or exceptions. We certainly need a list of primary and secondary contacts to be made when trying to get in touch with parents. I have never felt like we were intruding on privacy rights when we asked or sought information to assist with providing a proper educational environment. Thus those individuals that enroll kids should be trained and experienced in seeking appropriate information and sensing if the responses are legitimate or not. For example, there is nothing wrong about asking for proof of residency and copies of court orders when a parent says an "ex" is not allowed to see or communicate with the child.

It all starts on day one, and day one needs to be handled well.

Other times, a student's needs change throughout the school year. When it seems like there is a change in the child's behavior, attitude, work pattern, or dress or there are other signals that things might be off kilter, we need to be well versed on how to talk to the student and the parent, so we are proactive and helpful. I remember once when a fellow teacher told me about a fifth grade boy who all of a sudden stopped doing homework, had a sad look about him, and often wandered around during lunch hour rather than play with his friends. She asked him what was wrong, but he wouldn't say. She told me about her concerns since I was his physical education teacher (and principal), and had daily contact with him. I had not noticed the same behavior in my setting. After class one day, I asked him to help me with something and we began to talk informally. Within minutes, he was telling me that his mom had left the family and he and his little sister were living with his dad. I shared that I lived with one parent for several years and how hard it was to understand what they were going through. Within minutes, the lad was in tears and we talked for the next hour. Before the day was over, I had a conference with his dad to let him know what was happening at school concerning the boy's attitude and progress. But most important, we talked about ways we could help—both the boy and the family. We talked about resources we could suggest for the child and for the parents. We talked about the impact on the sister, and we extended a hand of assistance.

In this situation, no one came to us; we went to them. We were proactive rather than reactive. We ventured into the family structure, where some fear to trek. We showed that we cared and wanted to help. From the very beginning, we were on the side of helping rather than judging. We assisted rather than regulated. It makes a lot of difference how you position yourself when it comes to families.

Another issue has to do with parental motivation. What really is their agenda? All of us have met the parent, parent wannabe, or stepparent, or parent-in-absentia that wants to position him or herself as the savior, the good guy, the one who cares. Often it is to impress the child; sometimes, it is because he or she can't take a stand against the kid. And sometimes it is just to spite another adult. Too often, the school becomes the victim of their nastiness and, as often, "the bad guy." These are difficult situations, and they can (and often do) stretch our patience. It pits one parent against another and puts us in the middle. Usually there are few legal issues involved, so resolutions are based on practical actions. There are three fundamental considerations when a situation like this happens.

- First, and foremost, establish that the child's best interest is the key to the solution.
- Second, gather all sides of the issue, not just one, before a solution is proposed.
- Third, be caring, but always be professional.

I have found that meeting with the problem parent individually, when he or she doesn't have someone to impress, is very helpful. I have also discovered that when you take the time to try to understand and just listen, he or she often takes the time to think and discover.

This is a good time to introduce the "8-Step Method to Successful Conferences." This process, if done with patience and practice, works well. I think it can be applied to just about anything—a one-on-one meeting with a parent, talking to another staff member, meeting with a boss, even at home. The principles are sound and the process makes sense. Sometimes the eight steps flow smoothly; sometimes they need to be implemented firmly. The situation defines the process in certain cases. Here is a thumbnail summary of the process.

Step 1. The Positive Greeting

Initiate the conference or meeting with as little sense of confrontation as possible. Establish a neutral and environmentally friendly meeting place. Keep the initial talk upbeat and off topic. Look calm and confident. Be pleasant no matter what.

Step 2. The Positive Statement

Begin the discussion by saying something positive about the subject of the conference. (Your son is not only a handsome young man, but he is also very polite.) Whatever you say must be true. The comment must be one that doesn't promote a conversation, but extends a compliment or positive thought.

Step 3. Listen

Once the issue is introduced, and the parent/participant is asked to share his or her concerns or thoughts, just listen. Be absolutely quiet, and as hard as it may be, listen intently. Demonstrate responsive apathy. Show no emotions. Only speak to clarify and do that sparingly and with no excitement.

Step 4. Careful Transition

Move cautiously from them talking to you talking. Make sure they have finished. If you need to clarify anything, now is the time. Thank them for sharing. Try to mean it.

Step 5. Confirmation

Confirm what was said. This doesn't mean agree, just confirm. Confirm that you both want what is best for all concerned. Find common ground. Correct erroneous information.

Step 6. The Action Plan

List the desired outcomes of all parties. Jointly discuss options to reach these outcomes. Be realistic. Discuss common outcomes. If none, the goal may be to continue the discussion with other parties involved. You must agree on some action. If you made or make a mistake, apologize. Get it off the table at this point.

Step 7. Closure

Close with a summary statement and ask for agreement. Outline the follow-up steps you plan to take or that you agreed on. Thank them again for bringing the problem to you. Leave with a handshake, escort them out, and be very positive.

Step 8. The Follow-Up

Immediately put into place ways to assure that you do what you said you would do. Follow up with a call or email to be sure the problem is resolved, or being resolved. Follow up one more time and be sure to thank the person again.

Summary of the "Eight Step Method to Successful Conferences"

1. Positive Greeting

2. Positive Statement
3. Listen
4. Careful Transition
5. Confirmation
6. The Action Plan
7. Meeting Closure
8. Follow-Up

Conclusion

Parents and families—we all have them and thus we think we understand them. But they could hardly be more different! There are, though, a few approaches that work with most. And while these concepts don't replace laws and legal restrictions, they do help us resolve conflicts with a heart rather than a hammer, with compassion rather than depression, and with love rather than rage. So, the next time a family situation comes to you, think about this list of suggestions:

- Treat them with respect and they will return the favor.
- Walk in their steps to understand their needs.
- Remember that most will do anything for their child.
- Ask "What would I want or do in the same situation?"
- Understand, assist, be fair, and do what is right for the child.

Case Study #10: The Adamant Parent

Claire Mellane is a first year teacher of seventh grade English. One of her students is Jenny Willets. The story begins when

Jenny's mother, Mrs. Willets, calls Miss Mellane and "asks" (demands) a conference that very day, immediately after school. When the mother arrives, she quickly embarks on a heated dialogue concerning a "zero" that Claire had given her daughter for "supposedly" failing to turn in an assignment within 24 hours after the student returned to school from an excused absence. Mrs. Willets claims her daughter turned the work in immediately upon returning to school and that Claire lost the assignment. Furthermore, the mother tells Claire that she has called two board of education members and has suggested that Claire be terminated for both dishonesty and conduct unbecoming a first year teacher.

Administrative Perspective:

Here are the facts as they are presented: Mrs. Willets is madder than a hornet. She has ambushed Miss Mellane with an accusation before giving her a chance to explain. The mother has already started a campaign to get Claire fired based on this one incident. Mrs. Willets apparently has a personal relationship with two board members. And, according to what we know, Claire has not been given any opportunity to respond.

Let's first talk about the teacher. From a practical point of view, I suggest that Claire remain calm. This is important. Do not get angry. Do not make excuses. In most cases, I would suggest that the teacher make an effort to thank the parent for coming to her with the problem, but this might be a stretch since the parent has already talked to board members.

Here is a script that might be most appropriate: "I understand your concern. I don't want Jenny to receive a zero either. The issue here seems to be when the assignment was handed in. Since you have involved other people in this situation, I would like to share this concern with my principal and get back to you." If Mrs. Willets agrees, then the plan has been established. If she demands you contact the principal at that very moment, the teacher should consider this option. Personally, I would jump at the chance of doing this if the principal has good administrative skills.

In dealing with the issue, the principal needs to be a good leader, thus a good listener. He should let Jenny's mother repeat her side of the story. He should then ask Claire what her normal procedures are for a student returning from an absence with an assignment. He should not ask her for specifics of this case, but should rather focus on school procedures and/or classroom rules.

The principal should not refer, repeat, or reflect on the fact that Ima has talked with two board members. He should focus only on the issue, which is the student's assignment. This will determine if the zero is valid or was given in error. He should tell Ima that he would like to talk to the student and to Claire and gets all of the facts before making any comment. The principal needs to stick to his guns and get Mrs. Willets out of the school. By handling the issue in this way, the principal lends no credence to the charges of dishonesty and the request for termination. The principal focuses on the student issue only.

The principal should also contact the district superintendent. This step is not usually necessary in a building level dispute of this nature, but, in this case, it is necessary since board members have been contacted. The superintendent's role in this matter should then be to communicate with the board members to assure them that this matter is being addressed through the proper chain of command.

Getting back to the teacher, it is critical that she take steps to protect herself and validate her side of the story. The teacher should show the principal all of the relevant documentation. In this case, good documentation would include a copy of the student handbook signed by student and parent, a report of how the teacher collects papers, and the processes that the teacher uses in grading and assessing students. And, if there is any chance that the teacher did overlook the paper when it was first handed in, she should share that possibility as well.

I see a few concerns from the superintendent's perspective. If the superintendent first found out about this situation from the principal, it means that neither board member contacted the superintendent. Communication between board members and the superintendent is key in this type of situation. No superintendent wants to be surprised that trouble is lurking around the corner or that some student's mother is bad mouthing the staff. And any good board member should have responded to Mrs. Willets with a question such as, "What did the teacher say when you asked her about this?" If Mrs. Willets replied, "I didn't talk to her; I went right to the top," then the board member should have directed her back to the teacher to discuss the situation. Board members need to direct concerns and questions through the established chain of command, starting at the point of concern. Then they call the superintendent, not the teacher or the principal, to inform her of the call and their response. This is good boardsmanship.

This issue may seem to be trite, but even so it needs to be put to rest properly and professionally. If not, it could fester and cost a first year teacher her job. If Claire is not sure about when she really did receive the assignment, she needs to admit it, apologize, fix the grade appropriately, and put into place better checks and balances. She doesn't need to make excessive excuses or extended apologies, just fix it and move on. If Mrs. Willets continues to unfairly push for discipline or removal based on this single issue, then the principal needs to get the superintendent involved to help him extinguish this fire.

What seems like a minor incident can sometimes turn into a major disaster if the parties cannot find Middle Ground. However, this situation could be a real learning experience for everyone involved from the teacher to the board.

OK, Brian, I defer to your viewpoint…

Legal Perspective:

Thanks, Jim. This scenario requires more practical advice than legal counsel, and I appreciate your comments in helping the teacher, administrative team, and board deal with this angry parent. There are, however, a few legal points that are important to discuss so that this situation does not become a complicated legal matter.

First and most important, there should be a written school or district policy governing make up work. At the very least, the teacher should have a class rule on this matter. From a legal perspective, it is extremely difficult for a school or district to enforce or defend an unwritten policy, procedure, or practice, especially when it comes to dealing with an angry parent. Absent a specific policy, the parent could argue that procedure for handing in a late assignment is unclear or that her daughter still has the opportunity to hand in the assignment. Second, and in the same vane, it is always important that all school procedures comply with state and federal law, although in this case it is highly doubtful that there is any law specifically on this point.

Since the issue here is whether or not the student handed in the paper, it is important for both the teacher and principal to carefully investigate this matter and document their findings. As Jim appropriately points out, the teacher should write out her account of the situation and the principal should interview the student and teacher and put his findings in writing. Careful, well-prepared documentation is often the difference between a school district winning and losing a court case!

Another thought that immediately comes to mind is the need for privacy in dealing with all student matters. For example, parents frequently drum up past situations where one student may have been given a break or cut some slack. The parent might argue that "when Johnny was absent last week, his mother said the teacher gave him extra time to turn in his assignments." Here, it is important for the teacher or administrator not to get drawn into the debate. Discussing how another student was dealt with violates that student's privacy rights under the federal Family Educational Rights and Privacy Act and corresponding state laws. In this situation, the teacher or administrator should refuse to discuss any aspect of another student's situation by simply informing the parent that "it is a violation of law for me to discuss another student with you."

While we are on the subject of privacy, it is important to note that the superintendent should advise the school board members that they are also subject to the privacy provisions of FERPA and possibly state law. Especially in a situation like this, where the parent has approached two board members, it is important that board members appreciate the fact that they should not discuss the situation with anyone, especially the newspaper or other media outlet. If the board members wish to discuss this matter amongst themselves, they should only do so at an officially called school board meeting and only in closed or executive session.

Case Study 11:
Putting Johnny in the Middle

Johnny is a ten-year-old, fourth grade student whose parents are divorced. Johnny's mom has legal custody, although both parents are involved in his life and education. Unfortunately, Johnny's parents do not get along, and they frequently try to put the school in the middle of their volatile relationship. Johnny's dad calls the school every day to see if Johnny is present and has arrived on time. Both parents frequently show up after school to pick up Johnny, each insisting that it is "his (or her) night." Both parents demand that they receive report cards and other school documents and insist that they have separate parent-teacher conferences.

Legal Perspective:

I will try to address this question first, Jim, as there are a number of legal concerns when it comes to parent custody issues. It is not uncommon for parents to put their children or the school in the middle of their post-relationship discord. Teachers and administrators must be careful not to address the situation based on emotion and should only react in accordance with the information and legal documentation that is available.

To begin the analysis, it is important to note that, generally, both parents have the right to participate in the education of their children. Additionally, it is usually the custodial parent who has the right to make educationally related decisions. To this extent, both parents probably have the right to copies of report cards, school notices, and other related documents. Given the fact that these documents are relatively inexpensive to mail, I suggest sending both parents their own copy of these materials.

The issues related to parent-teacher conferences and the father's daily phone calls are more difficult to address. With the divorce rate at nearly fifty percent, having separate conferences for both parents could dramatically increase a teacher's workload. However, insisting that parents attend the same conference could make for an extremely uncomfortable situation. Additionally, the father's daily phone calls are time-consuming for school staff members and will quickly become annoying. Fortunately for me, these are not legal issues, *per se*, and I therefore leave them for my learned co-author to address below.

The question of who has the right to pick Johnny up from school does, however, have significant legal implications. If a school employee releases a child to the wrong person and the child is injured, kidnapped, or worse, the employee and school district may be partially liable. Here, again, it is critical for teachers and administrators to only proceed in accordance with the legal documentation that is available.

In order to head off the situation before it becomes an issue, school officials should insist on knowing who is allowed to pick up the child from school. This information may be contained in school registration materials. It is also strongly recommended that school officials obtain a copy of the parents' divorce decree or custody arrangement at the time the child is registered for school.

School officials should only act in accordance with the aforementioned documentation, unless one of the parties presents a more recent court order or both parties agree in writing to a modified arrangement. However, it is important to note that school officials may not act in accordance with an agreement by the parents to the extent it conflicts with official court documentation.

It is also important to notify applicable school staff of the pick-up arrangements for the child, especially if there are on-going problems. This notification should include the student's current teachers and any other staff members that monitor students after dismissal. If the "wrong" parent shows up at school to pick up the child, or if both parents show up and demand the child, never hesitate to contact local law enforcement to help mediate the situation. However, in doing so, make sure that the child is removed from the conflict and is not exposed to this potentially volatile situation.

Administrative Perspective:

Thanks for the legal assistance with this one because sometimes, in these cases, falling back on the law is the best course for all involved. Here is a common situation that makes this point. Mom is a royal pain to work with but has legal custody. Dad is a delight and very supportive of the school, his children, and the system. He always seems to comply. It would be easy to agree to a suggestion by Dad and turn a deaf ear to Mom even though the documents specifically give the decision-making power to Mom. Thus, knowing what the legal documentation on file says may prevent a possible problem and makes it easier to say "no" to the one who seems to be the parent who makes the most sense.

So how do you sort out all the legalities, anger, and craziness? How do you do what is right for the student, follow the law, and keep track of the parents, stepparents, boyfriends, girlfriends, half-friends, and in some cases, certified idiots? My suggestion comes from a long list of near hits, some misses, and one or two total failures to communicate, not to mention an attempted abduction and a couple of instances when a half-wired parent made a last minute (and I mean as the bus is pulling out) demand. Experience is a good teacher, but it is our hope that the readers use our failures and near misses rather than building their own database of fiascos!

Here is my first (and maybe best) recommendation. The instant it becomes evident that a separation or divorce is happening, or when two or more parents, from different directions, seem to be involved in the life of a child, the administration calls for the completion of a "Guardian Data Report." Call it whatever you want, but this report asks for, and gets, information signed by all involved parents, guardians, or custodians, and it includes any legal documentation that involves the child in any manner.

The "Report" should include all the basic information like the residence of the student for *each day* of the week, addresses and contact information of all involved parties, a summary of who is the custodial parent(s), transportation information, and a checklist clarifying who gets what, who will do what, and who is to be contacted and when.

The wording of the document can steer the preferences of the school without violating the rights of the parents. An example would be the following questions: Who will be attending the scheduled parent-teacher conference? If the named parent/guardian is unable to attend, who is approved to attend in his or her place?

Another "directing" statement might be the following: Unless a different address is listed below, report cards and all communications regarding meetings, attendance, discipline, and matters of general notice will be sent to the primary resident address listed at the top of this report.

A general statement might be included to assure that everyone understands the importance of the information provided. Please note that the information on this report will govern regular procedures and decisions concerning the safety and welfare of the student(s) so named, their transportation and release to adults, and related issues. If a dispute results from the information provided, or with any family member, third party, or the student, it may be necessary to involve legal authorities to resolve the issue(s).

And, of course, the "Report" must contain all legal directives. A statement such as the one that follows puts the onus on all parents or guardians to comply: All current and legal directives from the court or from other legal entities must be attached and updated as changes are made. This is the responsibility of the parents/guardians.

In order to provide consistent enforcement of the information on this report, copies must be shared and maintained by all school staff involved with the security, safety, and monitoring of the students named.

The information on this report must be verified and confirmed by the signatures of each parent/guardian so named on the report and must be **reconfirmed** when any change is shared.

This report can be modified or expanded to include a list of approved people who may pick up or deliver the child; the names of emergency contacts should be listed by the primary parent and guardian with any special notations per the unusual situation of the families.

If the principal is not able to obtain the needed information and signatures, a member of the central office should assist. A copy should be provided any teacher who is involved with grading, monitoring, or instructing the student, as well as copies to playground staff, district security, bus drivers, and monitors, plus, of course, administration.

It is imperative that principals notify all staff members immediately of students who have information of this nature on record. I suggest that teachers identify the student in the grade book or through some individual method so that they remember that the student is involved with a special situation family. Sometimes things go so smoothly that the staff gets negligent and then all hell can break loose and dangerous situations can result.

The practical administration of special family situations can be time-consuming and often wear heavily on your patience. Listening to a parent vent about the other parent, their family life, the stress involved, or how hard it is to work, raise a kid, and deal with an ex can be very stressful. One must tactfully listen, nod, and refocus on the practical needs of the student. Teachers and administrators must remind parents that it is our job to provide a learning environment free of as much discord as possible and constantly encourage the parents to work out the situations outside the parameters of the student and school as much as possible. It is also reasonable to remind parents that you do not have the time or capability to duplicate all conversations unless absolutely necessary, and even then, a reasonable time limit and schedule must be maintained. An offer to write key points of any conference and share that written report may suffice in place of actually meeting at two separate times. Mailing duplicate report cards usually only involves adding a second address to the report card distribution database and should not be considered an unreasonable request.

I firmly believe that if a parent brings the family dispute to the attention of the teacher, asks for unusually strange requests, asks for the teacher to testify on his or her behalf at a custodial hearing, or brings something bizarre to the table, the teacher should quickly and decisively refer the parent to the administrator for a procedural decision. A good administrator will listen, confer, advise, and try to mediate a reasonable course of action. When in doubt, this is a good time for the administrator to indicate that he/she needs to check with the legal advice of the district in order to follow proper procedures. It may be necessary to state that this is a first time request or a highly unusual one.

When school employees are put in a position of making a decision that is not clearly covered by approved procedures, they must use their best judgment concerning the welfare of the child with little worry about the consequences. If an out-of-town dad stops by the office and says he wants to personally deliver a gift to his child, I suggest you make an effort to contact the custodial parent and get permission first. If you can't, you might indicate that you have no signed approval on file for such a meeting and share the responsibility of getting the approval from the custodial parent with the unexpected guest—thus avoiding becoming the "bad guy." I have found it necessary to hide kids from parents, call the police to meet the parent, and have even kept kids off the bus when I suspected the presence of a parent who was listed under the "no contact allowed" category. Sometimes you err, but at no time did I have a custodial parent ever get angry over a mistake that was made in the name of safety.

Finally, split families and parents that can't get along are hardest on kids. Parents sometimes don't think beyond their own situation and forget the embarrassment or uncomfortable situation they create. Never forget that you have guidance counselors and social workers and others to help the kids, you, and the staff deal with the distress. And, as always, get legal support to steer you in the right direction when the answer is not clear, reasonable, or appropriate.

Case Study #12: Mrs. Zoliot and the Missing Undies

Mrs. Zoliot, the parent of a kindergarten-age child, insists on sending her daughter to school without underwear. The child's teacher, Ms. Davis, is appalled and provides the child with underwear on a daily basis. The parent is now calling and complaining that the new underwear "bothers" her daughter and that it is the reason she does not send the child to school with this item of clothing in the first place.

Legal Perspective:

Believe it or not, this, too, is an actual situation that I have had the pleasure of dealing with. It may seem trivial, even comical, but to all involved, it was anything but.

This is a case where the attorney and administrator have very clear roles and need to work as a team. It is the administrator's job to listen to the parent's concerns and try to work out an amicable situation that works for this student and does not jeopardize the health and safety of other students and school personnel. If such a solution cannot be arrived at, it is then the job of the lawyer to advise the administrator as to the exact state of the law and help the administrator to implement a legally sufficient response that will hold up in court should the parent seek judicial redress of the problem.

From a legal perspective, this is a relatively uncomplicated case. Students do not have a constitutional right to go to school. Students do have a right to receive an education, but this right is more or less a **property** right, as opposed to a **constitutional** right. Because we are not dealing with a constitutional right in this case, the school district can place parameters on a student's ability to attend school, as long as there is a reasonable educational reason to do so and the student had been provided with adequate due process.

Here, I believe that it is an inherently reasonable requirement that students are required to wear underwear to school. Not only is this a reasonable dress code requirement, with a kindergarten-age child, it becomes an important health and safety requirement as well. The school is therefore well within its rights to require the child to wear underwear to school. If the parent refuses to comply with this directive, the child can be banned from school attendance until such time as she wears underwear.

Lastly, if there is a medical reason that would prohibit the student from wearing underwear—and I have no idea what that would be—then the school is probably obligated to look at alternative methods of educating the child. In doing so, the school district would have great authority in determining what the alternative placement would be, provided it meets the minimum education requirements of the law of the particular state. In Illinois, for example, the child could be placed on homebound instruction, which requires the school to provide education by a certified teacher at least one hour a day when school is in session.

Okay, Jim. Try to keep a straight face while you solve this one!

Administrative Perspective:

There are so many directions I could take with this one that I don't know where to begin. Mostly because we are lacking a great deal of information.

First of all, the child (let's call her Peri) is in kindergarten. Let's assume a couple of things. First of all, I would think it is reasonable to assume that her Mom doesn't send her pantyless daughter to school in a skirt. If she does, Mom has a real problem. Thus, I am making the assumption that Peri comes in jeans, shorts, or pants. If Mom does send her to school in a skirt with no underwear, then this is a done deal. Tell Mom one of the basics in life, that people can't, at any age, display their "private" areas in public. Case closed, end of discussion. (If Mom fights this, have her locked up.)

Next, let's assume (and I think it is a reasonable assumption) that she is potty trained—able to control her elimination process. If this is true, then how did Ms. Davis find out about the missing apparel? It gets more immediate and complicated if the condition is visible or the child has lost control during school hours. And why is the mother calling?

Also, why would anyone call a lawyer about this situation unless Mrs. Zoliot threatened legal action against the school because they demanded Peri wear underwear.

Let me answer the questions as best I can. If Peri has a potty problem, she needs to wear underwear or Huggies. I agree with Brian that wearing underwear for this purpose is not something that has to be in the dress code. It is assumed, and appropriately so.

On the other hand, and this is a fair statement, if Peri doesn't have a potty problem and her lack of undergarments does not alter the safety or sanity of the school room, then what is the argument? Just because the teacher might freak out about it, can it be proven that it is a distraction or health issue if the lack of undergarments isn't known? Certainly it can be argued that if other kids know about it and give Peri a problem by making fun of her, this is a concern. But I have to wonder, do we do check all kids and staff to see how many don't wear undies? So this opens the door to question two: How did Ms. Davis discover the condition? If it was due to a sanitary situation, a hygiene condition, or humiliation from other students or something overt and public, then grounds are evident for a discussion with the mother. If she accidentally noticed the situation when in the restroom, or when tucking in Peri's shirt after recess, or by some other "incidental" activity, then it might be more the teacher's issue than Peri's. Again, we just don't know the answer to this question.

So, we can't answer why Ms. Davis called Mrs. Zoliot, but we do understand two things about the call: (1) Mrs. Zoliot is fully cognizant of the situation, and (2) the mother feels that her solution is appropriate for solving the problem that Peri is experiencing from wearing underwear. So we have now entered the dicey arena of messing with motherhood. Mom has allowed Peri to go without underwear, and the teacher has said it isn't permitted in her classroom.

Can this situation be resolved simply by the placement of one tiny pair of panties on Peri's behind? Or, will this issue eventually find its way to the Supreme Court?

Mom says, "No underwear, it bothers her." Ms. Davis says, "My students must wear underwear!" The line has been drawn, and Ms. Davis crosses it by telling Mrs. Zoliot that her daughter cannot come to school unless properly protected with underpants. Mom says, "You (the school) have no right to determine the underwear status of my child! Peri is not missing school!"

Ms. Davis contacts her principal. She, in turn, calls the school lawyer to share the issue and to ask for advice. The lawyer, immune to silly situations, suggests exactly what Brian has at the beginning of this caper—"try to work out an amiable solution." Sit down and list the concerns of each party and possible alternatives. Discuss the fact that you do not want Peri ridiculed by her classmates, embarrassed by any related problem, or in any way compromised by a health issue. The principal may even research and share some medical opinions about the benefits of underwear, and/or options to offer about alternatives (baggy underwear, boxer shorts, silk underwear, canvas underwear, etc.). No matter, the principal needs to bring compassion to the table since Mom is probably dealing with a little girl who says, "I'm NOT wearing that scratchy, uncomfortable underwear!" It may simply be a situation where the kid rules. But it also could be a situation where clothes are too tight or too rough—or where the girl reacts to specific materials or textures. Another viable solution is to allow Peri a day or two off while Mom takes her to the doctor for an exam or to offer homebound instruction while a solution is determined. Most parents cringe at the thought that their kid will be taught at home, even for an hour or two a day, and then left there for them to watch and help with their homework!

Here is the bottom line on this one—pun intended. Talk with the mom. Be understanding but forthright. Make it clear that you need to find a solution to the problem. Be creative, but don't call the lawyer or the superintendent or tell anyone else unless you cannot find a solution between teacher and parent. This is a kindergarten kid, and it isn't a national crisis. Don't make it one.

One more thing, if you can't find a reasonable solution, and if Mom won't work toward finding an answer you can all live with, then you probably have the first chapter of more Zoliot problems to come…

“Ignorance of the law excuses no man..”

John Selden

Chapter Nine

Managing Money and Student Activity Accounts: Brother Can You Spare a Dime?

Jim Burgett

Introduction

I'd like to subtitle this chapter "How to Avoid Brian" or "Ways to Keep Your Photo Off the Post Office Bulletin Board."

A couple of years ago, a school administrator I knew, and a "leader" in administrative organizations throughout his state, was suddenly and sadly very famous. It seems authorities went to his home and found a suitcase stuffed with cash. I'm not talking about a handful of single dollar bills; I'm talking hundreds of thousands of ones. It seems the guy was bilking his district right in front of his board and doing it with the unknowing cooperation of support staff and even some banks. No one caught on to his scheme of making a few (hundred thousand) bucks on the side. This wasn't a case of scraping a few dollars from the soda machine coffers. This was high stakes criminal activity that landed the fellow, alongside many of his state's previous governors, in prison.

I also knew an office clerk that used to redirect some athletic revenue into specific accounts in one bank and then redirect them again, and again, until they landed in her bank and her account. Although I'm not sure of the final figures in this case, we are talking about a ruined career, a bankrupt family, restitution, and prosecution that practically cost her everything.

And then there was the principal who diverted a few bucks from the soda machine now and then to pay for meals and other expenses that his high school students incurred when they traveled on field trips. It was potentially a legitimate use of the funds, but he kept no records, skimmed cash from the machines, handed the coaches and/or sponsors money when they left on the trips, and literally had no record of any of the transactions. When the process came to light, he was reprimanded by the board, hand slapped by the administration, and speculated about by the community. Even though his reputation was tarnished, those who knew him gave him the benefit of the doubt. However, it was the doubt that branded his career until he retired. Was he, or wasn't he, ethical? Did he, or didn't he, do what was right for kids? No matter what happened, if his name came up, there was doubt. And why didn't the district fire him, charge him, or do something substantial to him? Are they trustworthy? Were they in on it? Is this "standard practice" at the old school house? You can hear the naysayers drinking coffee at the local eatery, can't you?

The bottom line in each of these situations is really that, the bottom line. Does it balance, does it follow standard accounting procedures, are there records, is every transaction approved, is there a check and balance system in place, and is every dollar accounted for? These are the kind of questions that demand, require, and need to be answered legally and emphatically by educators everywhere.

Every "code of ethics" for educators, whether for teachers, administrators, board members, or non-certified employees, lists honesty and integrity as benchmarks. Legal and moral procedures are not options in our business. They separate those that are respected from those that shouldn't be. And it isn't good enough to say things like, "I'm a school principal, not an accountant," or "I never took a class in bookkeeping or money management; all my classes were in adolescent psychology and curriculum development." Nonsense. I never took a class in culinary arts or restaurant design, and yet, in my first administrative job, I ran the biggest and busiest restaurant in three towns. I never took a course in auto mechanics or transportation management, and yet I was responsible for the purchase, maintenance, and operation of the largest fleet of vehicles of any business in my district.

In our job, we are charged with so many different tasks in so many different areas that we need to know what to know, and we need to make sure we have procedures and personnel in place to make sure we do it right. That's why we hire cafeteria managers, nutritionists, bus mechanics, and bookkeepers. That's also why we insist on audits, inspections, and reviews. I never feared any inspection or audit because I always wanted to know three things when the reports came in: (1) Am I doing the job the way it should be done? (2) Can I do the job better? and (3) Do I have the right staff on board?

If one of the staff members in your office accidentally deposits the receipts from a bake sale into the football fund rather than the foosball fund, and no one catches it until the annual activity fund audit, done in mid July, the world will not come to an end. If, however, the Pepsi man delivered 900 cases of soda and fruit drinks to the district, all signed for and acknowledged, and only $225 of revenue was collected and audited, you have a problem that isn't so sweet.

Few schools operate without the supervision of a financial official or director. Small schools may double up the responsibility of money management between a superintendent, who also serves as a business manager, an office accountant, and/or a bookkeeper or a computer program that is tied in with a third party system. No matter how it is done, the major financial program usually operates under a predetermined state-approved system that is regularly and responsibly audited by a district auditor, treasurer, and/or accountant to make sure that the big bucks are handled correctly. Messing with these systems and controls is usually hard to do and always risky. When mathematical errors happen, they are frequently unintentional and correctable. However, when people write down fictitious information relating to attendance, program enrollment, lunches served, or other numbers that generate reimbursement, we are not dealing with a low IQ in mathematics; we are dealing with a moral deficit. Remember the discussion about branding? Remember how districts lose the trust of their constituents? Cheating is cheating, and when it happens, all sorts of repercussions can result from loss of faith to loss of employment to loss of freedom.

There are many suggestions to monitor the "in-house" monetary transaction, such as student activity funds and cash collections (lunches, fees, etc.). A few simple ideas that make sense for every school in every state are as follows:

1. Use the same fiscal year and fiscal accounting procedures for "in-house" funds as you do for district operations.
2. For student activity funds, use only one checking account for all funds but maintain individual detailed records for every account.

3. Always require proper documentation for every transaction, with copies for the office and for the individual responsible for the account. Copies must be filed and saved.
4. Every check a school writes should have two signatures.
5. Reconcile every account monthly.
6. Never permit overdrafts.
7. The opening and closing of any account must be approved by the Board of Education.

Accounting and administrative controls are a system of checks and balances that every administrator needs to understand. Administrators also need to know that every member of their staff follows accepted district, state, and federal budgeting, bookkeeping, and accounting procedures. Annual and periodical audits will help with not only the assurance that this is happening, but can help with the understanding of operational processes. Good auditors do more than count and tally; they suggest, teach, and advise.

One more suggestion is to follow the ABC's of in-house accounts and fund procedures. A stands for authorization, B is bookkeeping, and C is custody. Each of these procedures has its own set of guidelines, each should have its own handlers, and each should be handled separately. This protects and assures the integrity of the school system.

When school administrators are hired (usually in the summer), audits are normally being completed. This is a good time to review the financial operations of the school, or the department, or the district. If there are questions or issues, the new administrator should know them and fix them at the start of his or her realm of leadership. The same is true with board members. Read and understand the district audit when you are elected (or before), so you know and can own the information. Also, every teacher, coach, class sponsor, or employee who handles ten cents of school money should understand and know the procedures and processes involved. Less than ten cents, they can take a bye.

One final situation I'd like to share. I remember a parent coming to my home one summer evening and telling me "off the record" that during the summer junior football league, many students sold discount cards to raise money for new uniforms. The amount reported by the coach was suspected to be hundreds of dollars less than the parents felt was actually turned in. There were no records to look at and no paper trail of who sold what. It was pure speculation on the part of the parent. Here is the kicker; the summer football league was not a school program, not even conducted on school property, but the coach was one the district's high school assistant coaches. The parent wanted to tell me "off the record" that I had a crook on my staff. No proof. No formal accusations. No opportunity for the alleged "crook" to redeem himself. All of this could have been prevented if the coach bought a $2.98 receipt book at Wal-Mart. With some simple record keeping, the coach would have been a good guy rather than a suspected felon. Far fetched? Absolutely not!

So, be careful with money. Follow professional guidelines. Always have two or more people involved with every step. Don't skimp on audits. Welcome inspections and inspectors. Demand prudence in all operations. Be blatantly honest and expect the same from everyone. Follow these rules, and you won't need to hire Brian to clear your name or your record. He doesn't need the work anyway.

Case Study #13:
The Infamous Barton Vending Machine Transfer

Principal Smith has been at the Barton Elementary School for many years. He has always had a discretionary fund from the district that has allowed him some revenue for refreshments at meetings, etc. He simply purchased the items locally and turned in the "charge" receipts to the district bookkeeper. He had to submit the receipts with a district form that explained the reason for the expenditure and that he approved the charge. However, due to budget cuts, the fund was eliminated. Principal Smith still thought it was great public relations to provide refreshments at events and didn't agree with the cuts. So he decided to take a few bucks out of the school's vending machine each month and use the cash to purchase the refreshments. He also used some of the money to continue to reimburse a few of his teachers for their incidental expenses when they went on field trips.

Annually the school district auditor justifies revenue and expenditure for all district-owned vending machines. This past July the auditor noticed that there was a sizeable discrepancy in one machine at the Barton Elementary School, and it appeared that money was missing. Since Principal Smith was the staff member assigned to monitor the collection and deposit of the revenues, all fingers pointed at him. The missing revenue was included in the annual audit report. Oops.

Administrative Perspective:

While this isn't a very cute or dramatic example of a real incident, it does fairly represent some of the problems that exist in money management in schools and school districts today, and it is an example of how easily someone can inadvertently get himself in a wad of trouble.

The principal really doesn't think he has done anything wrong. And, to be honest, since the district superintendent hasn't yet read the audit, Smith doesn't even know that anyone else thinks he has done anything wrong either. To be honest, he thinks he is doing the right thing by using some of the school's revenue to provide incidental items that promote good will and a "caring" atmosphere. A few cans of soda and some bags of chips for the PTO and student council meetings are just a nice thank you for taking the time to be involved. And the few bucks he gives teachers for their lunch on a field trip to the zoo, or other incidental expenses throughout the year, don't amount to a hill of beans. Twenty or thirty bucks a month from the juice machine is peanuts in terms of the good will it buys, and he doesn't use the money for anything else, keeps it in an envelope in his desk, and never dips into it even for a candy bar when he stays late. What could be wrong?

What do you call this? Oh, yeah, rationalization. Well, Principal Smith, let me give you another perspective. The estimate you have of $20-$30 was pretty close. In nine months, you skimmed off $285 from the juice machine, according to the auditor, and that assumes that the delivery of product and collection of money have no other discrepancies. The money you turned in was counted and received by a no-nonsense bookkeeper in the Barton office, with the cash and a copy of the receipt sent to another no-nonsense record keeper in the unit office, who keeps the books for the 19 vending machines owned and operated by the district. According to district policies, the acceptance, counting, depositing, and recording of the funds were done under district accounting rules. Smith even received a copy of the receipt. He even keeps them all in a folder titled "Juice Machine." The record keeper deposits the money from the vending machines into the district's extracurricular activity account, and it is used to purchase equipment for either athletic expenses or playgrounds, all according to board policy. Seems like everything matches the accepted and responsible rules and procedures of the district, everything except for the tiny fact that Principal Smith is stealing money off the top!

There are six other machines located throughout the district that are owned and operated by the Booster Club. The product is put into the machines by the distributor, just like the school machines. Unlike the district machines, however, the Boosters pay the distributor a small percentage to count and collect the money, so the only thing the Booster Club gets is a check for their percentage of the profit. They don't get as much as the district because they elect to have the distributor do all the work. They also have to rely on the distributor's honesty in reporting the profit earned. The school district, on the other hand, allows the distributor to fill the machines and bill the district for the product, but the district has assigned certain people in each building to be responsible for the money collection and overall operation of the machines. The district's profit is substantially higher that way, unless, of course, someone skims the money first.

On the surface, it looks as if the rules are in place and the school is actually doing things right. The problems here are twofold. There is no immediate check on the profit ratio of each machine since it does not appear that the district compares product expense to revenue collected by machine. Remember, all the machine revenue was deposited into one account. The second problem is that there is no double check on the collection. This could be done if the money was collected in a locked container and the container emptied and counted in the office, or if the machine had a way of electronically counting money collected. Another method is simply to have two people collect and count the money and sign off on a form when it is turned in. A final, simple idea is to have Principal Smith collect and count the money and turn it in with a form that he signs that verifies this is the amount of money that he collected and counted. If he did this, he is then admitting to deceit.

You see, there are ways to keep everyone honest, and they need to be in place, followed, and monitored.

Back to the situation. Here are the facts, and only the facts. During the last fiscal year, $285 were not accounted for regarding the Barton School juice machine. Principal Smith is the designated person responsible for the fund collection of this machine. The audit has included the financial information in the formal report, printed and ready for distribution to the Board of Education (and public). The audit only gives the financial data and does not include the name of the person responsible, but it does list the discrepancy in its summary findings. Even Jimmy Olson at the *Daily Planet* could find out the name of the person responsible.

So what happens now? Well, if I were the superintendent and my auditor did not talk to me personally when the missing money was discovered, and before the audit was published, I would be beside myself, which would make two superintendents in one room—and that can be a problem. I would like the information so I could do some investigative work before it became a huge issue. There may a reasonable explanation that trumps the concerns of inappropriate behavior. There may indeed be a principal like Smith who doesn't get it or has a new interpretation of the word ethics. I want the chance to make that decision for myself. That is what the board is paying me to do. I also want to review procedures and understand why this happened in the first place. A missing $285 is not going to cause the school to be surrounded by federal agents, but it does raise several flags of concern and is enough to do a lot of individual and "corporate" damage.

Next, I want to confront the principal for an explanation. If he has one (which he does), I want to hear it and decide what to do about it. Let's assume he simply says the truth, admits that in hindsight it was not the right way to handle things, coughs up a check for $285, and says he will gladly give up the duty of juice machine honcho in the future. He apologizes for his error in judgment, and you weigh his excellent record as a principal and decide to let the issue pass with a hearty discourse and the fact that an adjustment in the account has been made to balance out the discrepancy. You share the facts with the board president or with the board in executive session. Case closed.

There are a couple of other ways this could end. Principal Smith could say he did not make an error, that the use of the money was appropriate to meet the public relation needs of his building, and thus earn himself a letter of reprimand, a request for total retribution, and a position one step away from the need to Google "resume construction" on his laptop. If the superintendent and board want to keep him, he may survive. If the event becomes public, he may need to go. This depends on a lot of factors. One thing in his favor is that he used all the money for school expenses.

The final solution I will discuss is the worst of all, but could happen. The superintendent simply accuses Smith of stealing the money and tells him to resign or face the consequences. He knows he did it, accepts the fact the superintendent will not instigate legal or criminal action if he resigns, and he does. Poof! Gone! And all over $285, with most of it redirected from one vending machine to another.

So, ladies and gentlemen, hear this plea. Don't take financial management lightly. Put into play solid procedures that can be evaluated, tested, and audited, and then don't mess with them. And share these stories with anyone and everyone who collects or counts one dime in your district. It is a fact that in a public institution there is a very low tolerance for anyone who messes with the money, no matter where it comes from. Trust me.

Legal Perspective:

Good advice, Jim. In the time that I have practiced law, I have dealt with a number of "Principal Smiths." And in each situation that I have dealt with, the principal, or superintendent, or teacher did not think that he or she was doing anything wrong. They were just "redirecting" some school district profits for a greater good. And, quite frankly, the explanations that most offered to me to justify their actions made pretty good sense.

Over the years, I have also dealt with a number of teachers and administrators who were, quite simply, bad money managers. They would go to Wal-Mart or another local store and purchase their local groceries and would pick up a few items for the school while they were out. Then the next Monday they would simply reimburse themselves out of the petty cash fund.

There were also the administrators and teachers who would use school district credit cards to purchase personal items, figuring that they had previously purchased school district items on their personal credit cards. No misappropriation intended, just an informal mechanism for settling the tab.

In fact, in all of the years that I have practiced law, I have never dealt with anyone who was intending to steal or mismanage money; however, in truth, they were!

There are two absolute no-no's in education: inappropriate relationships with students and fiscal mismanagement. The first of these is self-explanatory. Fiscal mismanagement, however, takes many forms. Trust me when I tell you that if money cannot be accounted for—to the penny—the **implication** is that the money has been stolen. And when there are no receipts, it is very difficult to create a paper trail to defend against charges of mismanagement or theft.

Below are a few tips to assure that you don't get into the same situation that Principal Smith and so many others have found themselves:

- Know state laws and district policies regarding management of student activity accounts, convenience accounts, and other financial accounts.

- All money should be spent for the exact purposes for which the money was collected.

- Make sure that all accounts are reconciled on a regular basis and make account balance sheets available to the school board.

- Three separate people should have an eye on financial transactions: one person should have authority to approve expenditures, one person should be responsible for bookkeeping and accounting, and a separate person should have custody of the funds.

- Require two signatures on all checks.
- Require receipts for reimbursements and maintain receipts for all transactions.
- Immediately document any account irregularities.

Chapter Ten

Accommodating Gay, Transsexual, and Other Minority Student Populations: It's a Small World After All

Jim Burgett

Introduction

It's a different world. I guess it all depends when you arrived on the planet as to how different it has become. Adapting to the differences that surround us is another issue, and it is directly related to that variable called flexibility. I don't mean touching your toes; I mean the ability to bend with the changes of the world.

As I write these words I am sitting in an airport with a typewriter on my lap, sans paper. It is an electronic version of what I grew up with. It's different from my old Corona. And I don't miss the experience of smacking the keys of that old device, hoping the arms that ended with the metal letters didn't collide when they popped up or that the ribbon didn't jam or, God forbid, find the end of the spool. No, this "typewriter" cost me close to three thousand dollars and does more things than I can list, do, or even pronounce. It's not a Corona; it's an Apple. Yes, I am writing on a thin electronic device named for some reason after a fruit. I am also watching a myriad of things happen around me.

Right down the aisle is a bank of corded pay phones, all lined up in neat little booths. No one is sitting in any of them, but about half the people I see are indeed talking on the phone—while sitting, walking, and multitasking. Mine is hooked to my belt receiving emails and baseball scores and, once in a while, a call from some distant place.

There's a guy three seats from me watching a movie from a little machine about the size of a checkbook. He has earphones on, but no cords. A lady across from me is either an alien or has had some form of cranial implant installed and may have experienced shock therapy. Why do I think these things? Well, she has what looks like a metal green bean, about two inches long, coming out of one of her ears headed toward her nose—and she is talking loudly to someone, but no one is there. I wonder if her device is called a Bean. If I can have an Apple, she certainly can have a Bean.

And then there are the people. I can see a number of families—you know, the ones that have a set of parents, one from each sex, and a couple of kids, all pulling cute little brightly colored suitcases with wheels and handles with Batman or some sort of Princess displayed on the side. There is a guy across from me who looks a bit discombobulated. I'm headed to Denver, then to Helena, Montana, where the forecast calls for snow and temps in the 30's. He is wearing flip-flops and a t-shirt that has some sort of group pictured on the front. The group looks like they are hugging each other and one member has just stuck a finger into an electric outlet. The man looks as frazzled as the group. He will look even more frazzled when he gets off at the airport and freezes his flip-flops. He has spiked green hair and a mass of things sticking in and out of his face, including his ears, nose, and lip—and that's just what I can see. He may have something sticking out of the top of his head, too, but he has a cap covering anything that may be stuck into his skull. How he got through the some-sort-of-ray machines we had to slide through at the security checks, I'll never know. Yep, it's a different world.

And there is more. I can see another couple, or at least they seem like a couple. I can see a little touching here and there, some cute smiles back-and-forth, both wearing wedding rings, both men. They seem to be enjoying life, and I would guess, or hope, they are headed to Denver or beyond for a few days of R & R. Who knows? I didn't ask.

I also see another couple. A man and a lady—each of a different skin color. They have a couple of kids. They look like every other couple I can see toting kids—a bit stressed. And yes, the kids have cute little suitcases they are pulling around and, on occasion, using as both seats and as a substitute for a soccer ball. I would guess they are headed home. The thrill of traveling seems distant.

Just 50 years ago, many of these things I have described would have been either extraordinarily rare in public or simply inconceivable anywhere. Telephones plugged into your ears. Watching Technicolor movies on your cordless checkbook. Portable computers. Any computers. Multi-racial families. Two people of the same sex showing open affection toward each other. Or the personal mutilation of metallic probes, rings, and spears poking the visible extremities of a live human, who also has spiked green hair.

Earlier, I mentioned the capacity to be flexible. You know, to have the ability to change with the times. To accept what you see, even if you don't understand, appreciate, or even like it. People like me, very mature and seasoned—old—have had to bend so many times I am surprised we don't all look like an Auntie Anne specialty. But bending is good.

Bending is the essence of being willing to learn. I am rather proficient on the things I carry with me, like my computer, my iTouch, my Blackberry (another fruit), my digital camera. All of these things allow me to work wherever I am, stay in touch, and create. Neat changes.

When I notice a couple who are of different races, I don't actually see that first anymore. What I look for is the interaction, not the color, accent, or cultural differences. I see two people, not two races. When I see a gay couple, while I don't really get it, I don't get all flustered and start the judging routine. I see two people, and if they are happy and adding to life's goodness, so be it. And even though I would rather have a lobotomy than have my tongue pierced, even though I truly don't understand the reason or rhyme of holes in the earlobes filled with discs the size of dimes or quarters or of pictures of the Mona Lisa, the Last Supper, or the Alamo inked in vibrant colors all over someone's torso (including his head), I have to remind myself that it is *his* head, not mine, and his right to be a walking art gallery. Although I do wonder what will slide off the table at the Last Supper when things begin to sag a few years hence.

What does all this rambling have to do with finding Middle Ground? Well, if you read it again, you will see that as the world has morphed into its present state of creative bliss, each of us has also morphed to a place of understanding and acceptance, or at the very least, tolerance. That suggests that most of us have transitioned over the years to the land of Middle Ground when it comes to the preferences of human choice. Most of us, at least.

Now let me mentally wander a bit more, maybe into terrain that might get me in trouble. I call it the "PC (political correctness) swamp." It is that mush of ground that we tread on carefully. It is the land of uncertainty, where personal opinion rules and where the rules are essentially made and broken with regularity. It is also the land where what is right, what is moral, and what is offensive are as elusive as sunshine in Alaska in January. It's that place where you wonder if it is okay to refer to an African-American as Black or a Black as an African-American. Where older folks still say Negro and do it with respect, and where a White man might prefer to be called a Caucasian, but a Mexican shudders at being called Latin-American. It's a place where lesbians may prefer the term "gay," and gay men may prefer to be called just men. If you call an Asian lady an Oriental, with full respect, you may offend her, but if you call a Korean an Asian, they may want to be called a Korean. It's a strange world. It's a place where we might offend when we mean to compliment, but say the wrong thing when we don't know what the right thing currently is. And for many of us, we just decide to say nothing and maybe that is the ultimate Middle Ground: when we just accept people as people. I don't know, but that it why this place is a swamp.

So while the world changes and while being politically correct is an art form rather than a science and while we are protected from all sorts of inappropriate behaviors or attitudes by a plethora of laws, we have, for the most part, found Middle Ground between acceptance and rejection. Don't get me wrong here. I'm not saying we've found moral standards that everyone has accepted. Nor am I saying that we have eliminated all forms of prejudice. And we certainly haven't agreed on what is universally acceptable behavior. We have made gains in tolerance and understanding when it comes to the rights of others. Thus, over time, we have come to accept green hair; new sexual preferences; tattooed foreheads; mixed racial, religious, or cultural relationships, and even behavior that we might consider bizarre…*if it is legal and does not infringe on the rights of others*.

"If you live in my house, you live by my rules" is a nice statement, but most people don't live in our house, and our rules are certainly just that, ours. To get along we have to go along.

The keys words for this chapter are tolerance and protection. Tolerating the *legal and non-disruptive* behaviors of others and protecting the rights of everyone. Accomplishing this is not always easy, but it is always interesting.

So, as educators, regardless of specific title, we now sing to a different tune. And, if you'll excuse the pun, not an "i" tune, but the tune of respecting the rights of others, even if and when those rights seem strange, hard to understand, or just plain goofy.

I'm not going to go legally ballistic here. That's my partner's job. I'm not even going to quote the United States Constitution or talk about discrimination or share legal rulings. I'm going to talk about pure and simple common sense. Brian has already outlined the ins and outs of freedom of speech. If it is generally offensive, or interrupts the learning process, it probably needs to be adjusted. If it involves the actual or possible safety of another human being or an institution, it probably needs to be adjusted. It's that simple.

We aren't as shocked by a student's sexual choices, or identity, these days as were past generations. Hopefully, we have learned to adjust and even tolerate these changes. What we can't accept is the intolerance that leads to cruelty or dangerous behavior. And, while everyone might not share the same level of understanding and tolerance toward others, let's hope we have all found Middle Ground when it comes to individual rights, including the right to be treated fairly and with respect.

Each situation needs to be reviewed on its own merit and unique circumstances, and no administrator, teacher, or board member should feel awkward about the fact that he or she may be facing a very different situation than he or she is used to. The same techniques take place here as they do when you had the first case of AIDS or the first time a teacher was arrested for some inappropriate act or the first building fire or the first of anything new or different. No matter what the situation, you still employ the following basic techniques: identify the issue, talk with the parties (and/or families), seek advice, and find a solution that protects the parties involved and preserves the right to be educated.

Our first case study might give some insight to what I have tried thus far to say. Life changes, so deal with it fairly and honestly. You might not understand it, but come to the table with an open mind and know that you need to retain safety, respect, and an environment conducive to learning.

Case Study 14:
Michael and Michelle, a Couple of One

Consuella Contos is the Dean of Students at Goldwest High for all kids whose last names are between Gur and Nom. One of her jobs is to enroll her assigned students, by appointment, during the first week of August. Kids 16 and older can enroll without a parent present. At 2:00 p.m. on August 5, CC (as the staff calls her) prepares for an appointment with a senior named M. Kertz. She pulls the record and remembers Michael Kertz from a few mandatory visits over the years. She recalls a nice young man, slight of build, with a solid academic record. He performed well on his ACT test, and it looks like his general liberal arts track could lead him into teaching or a similar profession. She sees no previous enrollment in athletics but a consistent history of participating in the band. She sees nothing unusual as she prepares for his visit. Oh, my, is she in for a surprise.

At exactly 2:00 p.m., there is a knock on CC's door, and there stands a very petite, well-dressed, cute young lady. CC politely asks if she can help her. The student replies, "I'm here for my appointment." CC responds, "There must be a mistake; I have another student scheduled for this time slot." The student replies, "Is it M. Kertz?" To which CC answers, "Well, yes, it is." And then the ball drops. The student announces, "I am Michelle Kertz, formerly Michael Kertz, and I am enrolling as a senior student, now female."

During the next few minutes, Michelle enrolls for classes and announces that she plans to begin the year not as a transsexual student, but as a female, and she fully plans to use female restrooms and locker rooms.

Administrative Perspective:

Let's assume CC is not a rookie. Let's even say she has been a Dean at Goldwest High School for 13 years and is second in seniority. Let's also give her kudos for being good at what she does and highly respected by students, staff, and families. But with all this said, let's also realistically assume she has never had a Michael one year become a Michelle the next. So CC sits there and really does not know what to say. Here are a few thoughts that enter her mind—and would probably enter yours or mine, too:

Is this a joke?

You can pass for a girl, and, in fact, you actually look like a girl, but what is really going on here?

Are your parents in on this little switcheroo, if indeed there was one?

If you are serious, did you, you know, have surgery?

And then CC starts to think professionally and she quickly comes up with a new set of questions:

- What can I ask? How do I remain professional and appropriate?
- Do I have the right to ask if she is a girl, or thinks she is a girl, or is planning to become a girl?
- Can I ask if we can call in her (his?) parents to talk about this?
- Do I just register now and deal with the bathroom and locker room question later?
- Is it too late to request a personal leave day that started at 2:00 p.m.?

The first round of shock and awe is over. Now it's time to handle the situation. Lots of issues, concerns, questions, and potential problems seep into CC's suddenly overstressed cranium.

She does what I feel is the right thing to do. She embraces her response with honesty, but not with desperation. She doesn't raise her hands in disbelief and yell, "Why couldn't your last name be Numchuck?" Instead she says, honestly, but emphatically, "Michelle, I have never been asked to register a transsexual or process the requests you are proposing. This is new to me, and while I want to be respectful of your request, I need some direction in how to handle it. A lot of questions come to mind that need to be addressed. I would like to put your registration on hold until I have time to discuss this with the principal. I will do that as soon as possible and call you for a new appointment for registration." If Michelle responds negatively to this answer, I would suggest CC hold tight and promise a call no later than noon tomorrow. CC knows that, at the best, she might be able to call earlier, and, at the worst, she can call by noon and set a date to register that gives enough time to get the pieces of this puzzle put together.

So Michelle is not enrolled, Michael is not dropped, and CC is almost doing a slow jog to the principal's office. And it only takes the principal a few minutes to digest the story before he calls the superintendent, who before the night is over has called the board president, with the information, but not the name(s). He tells the board president that until he is advised by the district's attorney, he would rather keep the name confidential. Welcome to the 21st century!

Here we are. CC is still recovering from shock and has advised the principal that Michael/Michelle has been promised a response no later than noon the next day. The ball is out of her court, and she is glad, to be honest. The principal has informed the superintendent and been promised a response by noon tomorrow, and the superintendent, in turn, has already placed a call to his district's legal counsel.

This situation is not in the board policy manual nor will it be easy to call a mentor or neighboring administrator to find help on the decision.

What would be helpful would be advice on the possible outcomes. Who might you know that has dealt with sexual discrimination, threats, or harassment? Who has dealt with student ridicule or group pressure or gay rights issues? What kind of help can you get if you ask someone from your association to post a third party request on the list-serve asking for the name of any administrator who has had this issue and would like to help. And, of course, Google searches will provide ample literature to help with the issue and decision making process, as I found out preparing for this case study.

My guess is that the district's lawyer is going to advise on a couple of the basic ideas. One, that sexual preference is personal preference and the school has no say in Michael's transgender status as Michelle. Yet, since this is a major issue, Michael's parents or legal guardians need to be involved in the decisions that follow. I would assume the call back to Michael (the one presently on the enrollment sheets) is a call for an appointment with him/her and the parents. Depending on the comfort of those involved and the recommendation of the lawyer, I would assume the meeting will only involve CC and the principal. I would also assume that Michelle will be enrolled and her request for use of the ladies restroom and locker room will be denied for several reasons: the first is the comfort level of the other students, and the second is that if Michael is still a biological male, a dress is not going to be a free pass into the ladies facilities. Unisex facilities or other concessions will need to be made to facilitate his/her request. This can get confusing!

During the enrollment and adjustment phase of this issue, all parties must reach some form of agreement on what the new Michelle can and cannot do, and the lawyer should be involved with the issues that are not clearly and positively agreed upon. However, once Michelle starts school on August 24th, it will be imperative that answers to questions, explanations to students and staff, and information to the nosey press need to be readied. It will also be very important that everyone be on the alert for harassment, humiliation, and discrimination. A clear outline of what and how these issues should be handled should be in place. I would also make sure that the parents are informed that you would like to see Michelle meet, on a regular basis, with a school psychologist or other appropriate staff member to help with the adjustment and the possible problems.

Everyone should be on the ready for both parents and students alike to make this a major concern. Plans should be made to hold administrative meetings for the purpose of brainstorming effective responses for anything that may come up.

Michael becomes Michelle. Bobby comes out of the closet. Darla invites Debbie to the prom. John wears a skirt to school. A movie like this is coming to your auditorium soon. Be prepared. Understand that it is not your place to change the orientation, but it is your place to make sure that rights are not violated, school is not disrupted, and people remain safe and healthy.

Legal Perspective:

Thanks, Jim. If we couldn't inject some humor, jobs in education would surely drive us over the edge. But this is one time when I must wear my serious hat…

The issue of student equality is one that is very important to me as a lawyer, and I hope it is equally important to every teacher, administrator, or school board member. All students, no matter what their race, religion, or sexual orientation, need to be treated with dignity and respect. To do otherwise violates the law and can expose decision makers to personal liability.

As an education community, we have a somewhat mixed record in dealing with issues of race and religion. I think we do a much better job as a whole dealing with issues of race and religion than we did 20, 10, or even five years ago—but we certainly have room to improve. Likewise, when it comes to dealing with GLBT—gay, lesbian, bisexual, and transgender—students, we have made some progress, but I am occasionally confronted with a situation where schools have treated these student populations with such abhorrent inequality that it concerns me a great deal.

Whether we like it or not, students come to us in different shapes, sizes, colors, and with different sexual orientations. It is not our job to question; it is our job to educate. This means that a gay or lesbian couple has the same right to attend prom as any other couple. It means that transgender students must not be discriminated against when it comes to participation in school activities. It means that a school or district must take seriously complaints of harassment against GLBT students and deal with such situations in a sincere and effective manner.

Back to the issue at hand. I imagine that most of us would have a difficult time handling this situation, for it is one where very few of us have had much experience. Yet, if the situation is handled incorrectly, it can become a complex, expensive, and time-consuming legal issue. But, if the situation is handled correctly, it will become a non-issue from a legal standpoint.

As Jim alludes to in his comments, Michelle must be enrolled as a student. And, yes, there are some unique considerations that must be taken into account, which include: (1) whether Michelle should officially be enrolled as a male or female, (2) which locker room and restroom facilities Michelle can use, and (3) whether Michelle will participate on the boys' or girls' athletic and intramural teams. These are tough questions.

In terms of whether Michelle is officially enrolled as a male or female, it depends, in part, on whether Michelle has undergone gender reassignment surgery. This same question is important in determining whether Michelle participates on the boys' or girls' athletic and extracurricular teams. In terms of which restroom and locker facilities a transgender student uses, I am generally okay in providing a separate facility, as long as this is done with a modicum of discretion and confidentiality.

Admittedly, a number of issues when it comes to GLBT students have yet to be determined. However, what is certain is that Michelle must not be denied any of the rights or opportunities that are made available to other students.

Chapter Eleven

Technology and the Schoolhouse: Trying to Keep Up with the Students

Brian D. Schwartz

Introduction

With the advent of the Internet and computer technology, today's students enjoy access to every corner of the globe. Communications that once took weeks are now literally instantaneous. It is a world far different from the one most of us grew up in. In most cases, it is an area where the student's knowledge far exceeds that of the teachers, administrators, and school board members.

In other chapters, we have examined some aspects of technology. For example, in Chapter Four we discussed the ability of school districts to discipline students for purely off-campus misconduct conducted through the use of technology. Likewise, in Chapter Six we discussed the importance of safeguarding student records in light of the informational age. The purpose of this chapter is to take a look at some additional aspects of technology in order to help teachers, administrators, and board members keep pace with students and the many technological issues that impact schools on a day-to-day basis.

Regulation of School Websites

Schools enjoy a great deal of authority when it comes to regulating school-created and -maintained websites. If the website is solely maintained by the school or district, a closed forum is created whereby the website may be used strictly for school purposes. However, much like the use of a school's grounds and facilities, a school may open up the use of its website to nonschool-related groups and to the public.

Once a school decides to open its website to use by outside groups, all similarly situated groups must be granted the same opportunities. For example, if a school allows a local civic group to post an event announcement to the school's website, all other community groups must be allowed to post announcements for their events. Additionally, the federal Equal Access Act (applicable to high schools) provides that student religious organizations must be granted the same access to school facilities as other student organizations, unless the school specifically limits access only to curriculum-related student organizations. The same principles undoubtedly apply to school website use by student groups.

In light of the above discussion, schools are wise to specifically delineate their policy for school website use. Schools may limit the use of the school's website to school-related materials and events (creating a closed forum), limit the school website to use by student groups (creating a limited public forum), or allow the website to be used by all community groups (creating an expanded limited public forum). Additionally, students should be told that the school has final editorial authority whenever students are given school credit for designing, editing, or updating the school's website.

Internet Filtering Software

The use of Internet filters is one of the most hotly debated topics in the area of technology law. The main debate focuses on whether such filtering mechanisms are a form of censorship and undermine constitutionally protected free speech.

The filter debate has been fueled by the federal Children's Internet Protection Act (CIPA). CIPA requires that, as a condition of receiving federal E-rate funds (grants to assist with technology costs), public school districts and libraries must certify that they have an Internet safety policy and technology protection measures in place. Such policies must include technology protection measures to block or filter Internet access to pictures that are obscene, child pornography, or otherwise harmful to minors.

CIPA was recently challenged as it applied to public libraries and was initially held to be an unconstitutional infringement on the First Amendment. However, in 2003, the United States Supreme Court reinstated the Act as it applies to public libraries. The Court stated that in order to fulfill their educational and cultural roles, libraries must have broad discretion to decide what materials to provide to their patrons. While CIPA has never been challenged as it applies to public schools, additional rulings by the Supreme Court would seem to invalidate any remaining questions of the Act's constitutionality as it applies to educational facilities.

At the same time in which schools are subject to lawsuits for censorship, others have been under scrutiny for failing to protect children from the harmful effects of the Internet. In light of the current debate on Internet filters, one might ask how schools might meet their obligation to protect students from harmful information found in cyberspace while at the same time keep from violating First Amendment guarantees?

The following tips are designed to assist school officials in maintaining adequate security and preserving student rights:

- Internet filters are not a substitute for schools diligently monitoring student computer and Internet use. Students should always be appropriately monitored to make sure they are complying with the school's Acceptable Use Policy and other school rules.

- When filters are used, the school should develop a filtering policy that is tied to student safety and the Children's Internet Protection Act. It is essential that all school policies are elucidated *before* they are challenged.

- School personnel should be given flexibility to determine what Internet material is offensive given the age of the students and other appropriate standards.

- All filtering devices should have a mechanism to disable the filtering software for bona fide research or other lawful purpose, provided the student or staff member has prior permission from the appropriate administrator.

File Sharing

File-sharing programs allow people to share files with others on the Internet. Although the concept of being able to share files on the Internet is a noble one, the process and the content involved in file-sharing have many pitfalls for schools. To understand the pitfalls that file-sharing holds for schools, it is important to know more about how the file-sharing programs operate.

A number of software programs are available that facilitate the file-share process, such as Kazaa, Shareaza, Limewire, Frostwire, and WinMX, to name a few. If a student or staff member loads a file-sharing software program on a school computer, it allows the user and the other clients that are a part of the file-sharing network to access all files that are resident on the file-sharing network's computers. It also allows the file-sharing network to utilize the client's computer to help run the file-sharing network, significantly degrading the function of the overall local area network due to the increased Internet traffic that file-sharing creates.

In addition to the network congestion, considerations related to file-sharing involve the appropriateness of content of the file-sharing and copyright considerations related to that content. File-sharing, depending on the configuration of your network, may allow for inappropriate material to be downloaded or accessed by students or staff. Also, some file-sharing downloads may be an infringement of copyright laws that could result in financial penalties for the school district.

To guard against the pitfalls of file-sharing, schools need to take preemptive steps. File-sharing by students and staff should not be allowed, as explicitly stated in the district's acceptable use policy. A school district's local area networks (LANs) should be equipped with software that monitors Internet traffic to detect any file-sharing within the LAN. Finally, school district policy should address software file-sharing downloads and copyright violations.

Acceptable Use Policies

Acceptable Use Policies, or AUPs, are an important element of any school's technology planning. AUPs serve not only to protect schools from liability, but place students and staff on notice as to rules, regulations, and expected conduct. AUPs differ dramatically in their scope and depth. Listed below are essential considerations in the development of an AUP for your school or district:

1. **Scope of Use**: Each school or district must determine what scope of use it will allow for students and staff. Most districts do not allow either students or staff to have unlimited access to the World Wide Web and include a statement in their AUP that Internet and email are solely for educational purposes.

2. **Rules for Usage**: Any good AUP for both staff and students states that Internet and email use is a privilege and not a right and that a violation of the AUP may result in termination of usage and/or appropriate discipline. The school's rules should also be clearly listed so as to provide adequate notice. Additionally, the appropriate discipline policy should be incorporated by reference so as to allow the school the full range of disciplinary options.

3. **Prohibited Uses**: The AUP should contain a statement that the school condemns any illegal use of the school's computer system, including the pirating of software, hacking, copyright violations, harassment or threats, defamation, and the like. Schools are also wise to consider the following prohibited activities: use of obscenities, viewing or downloading pornographic materials, sharing account information or attempting to use another person's account, file-sharing or downloading

file-sharing programs, harming school property, attempting to bypass or bypassing the school's filtering system, or participating in any other activity that is detrimental to students, the school, or school officials.

4. **Liability**: The AUP should include a provision that the school does not guarantee the reliability of the data connection and does not verify the accuracy of information found on the World Wide Web.

5. **Property / Privacy Statement**: A statement should be included in the AUP that all information sent or received from a school computer, including email, are school district property, should not be considered confidential, and may be accessed by school personnel at any time.

6. **Training Sessions**: Some schools have experimented with mandatory training sessions for both students and staff before allowed access to the Internet or assignment of an email address.

7. **Agreement Provision**: It is recommended that both students and staff sign a document indicating that they have read and understand the appropriate AUP and agree to abide by the terms and conditions contained therein. Students and staff should also agree in writing to indemnify the school or district against any losses or damages that occur out of violations of the AUP.

8. **Parent Permission Form for Student Use**: Many schools also require parent approval before students are allowed to use the Internet or the school's email system. It is recommended that any parental permission slip also contain a

statement whereby the parent agrees not to hold the school, district, or school personnel responsible for any material the student accesses or transmits via the school's computer system.

Student and Staff Email Use

A growing number of students and school staff members have electronic mail or email addresses that are routed through the school or district's technology network. Furthermore, many students and staff members are able to access their respective email accounts from home computers or other computers that are off school property. This use of email has created two primary concerns for schools and school districts: user privacy and sexual harassment through the school or district's email server.

Any discussion of email privacy in schools starts with the Electronic Communications Privacy Act, or ECPA. Adopted in 1986, the Act is part of the federal wiretapping statutes and deals with the way schools and other entities monitor electronic mail. Specifically, the Act makes it a criminal offense to intercept electronic mail while such mail is in transit.

There have been at least two important federal appellate court decisions that have provided clarity to the Act as it applies to schools. In *Steve Jackson Games, Inc. v. U.S. Secret Service*, the Fifth District Appellate Court held that Congress did not intend for "intercept" under the Federal Wiretap Act to apply to "electronic communication" when those communications are in "electronic storage" within the provider's system. Additionally, in *Pollock v. Pollock*, the Sixth Federal Circuit held that as long as a parent or guardian has a good faith basis for believing that it is in the best interest of the child, the parent or guardian may vicariously consent on behalf of the child to the recording of a telephone conversation. Many school law experts believe that the *Pollock* decision would naturally extend to student email.

However, despite the latitude granted to school officials in viewing staff and student email, students and especially staff may still have a reasonable expectation of privacy in their email communications. Therefore, schools are wise to take the following steps: clearly outline that there is no expectation of privacy in email communications that are accessed or delivered through the school or district network, allow school officials to access email communications at any time, and limit email use to school purposes. These steps are most effectively taken through the acceptable use policy. Staff members and students (along with their parents) should always sign a copy of the AUP or documentation acknowledging the aforementioned privacy waiver.

Sexual Harassment through Email

Schools and school districts have seen increased liability in the cases of employer to employee, employee to student, and student to student sexual harassment. The use of email has provided another avenue for sexual harassment and has increased the responsibility of educational institutions to deal with this problem.

Most cases of sexual harassment against schools and districts are brought in federal court under either Title VII of the Civil Rights Act of 1964 or Title IX of Educational Amendments of 1972. Title VII provides, in part, that it is unlawful to discriminate against someone in an employment capacity because of the person's race, color, religion, sex, or national origin. This statute protects employees from sexual harassment from supervisors or other employees. In order for a district to incur liability, the victim of the harassment must show that the harassment was done under the guise of employment and that the district knew about the situation—or should have known—and failed to take reasonable action.

Title IX protects students and provides, in part, that no person on the basis of sex may be denied the benefits of or participation in the educational process. In order for liability to ensue against the school or district, the victim must show that the sexual harassment was objectively offensive, that the school or district had actual knowledge of the situation, and that the school or district acted with deliberate indifference in failing to diffuse the situation.

In lawsuits brought under either Title VII or Title IX, the law imposes on the victim the burden of proof. What constitutes constructive or actual notice by the school or district is frequently a subject of litigation. Written email communications presented to school officials may aid in establishing such notice, whether actual or constructive. The victim's continued receipt of such harassing email through the school or district's network may further establish that the school or district failed to take the appropriate action.

A Word on Copyright Law

Although a complete discussion of copyright law is beyond the scope of this book, there are a few comments that should be noted regarding student and school use of copyrighted material from a digital medium perspective. Copyright law extends to all original works of authorship, including software programs, CD-ROM, and web pages. Additionally, it is no longer required that an author place notice on the document or register it in order to receive all of the rights enumerated by the federal Copyright Act.

There are two important exceptions to the Copyright Act as it applies to the educational setting. The fair use doctrine provides that the "the fair use of a copyrighted work, including such use by reproduction in copies or phonorecords or by any other means specified by that section, for purposes such as criticism, comment, news reporting, teaching (including multiple copies for classroom use), scholarship, or research, is not an infringement of copyright." There are four specific factors to be applied in determining whether or not a particular use violates copyright law: (1) the purpose and character of the use, including whether such use is of a commercial nature or is for nonprofit educational purposes, (2) the nature of the copyrighted work, (3) the amount and substantiality of the portion used in relation to the copyrighted work as a whole, and (4) the effect of the use upon the potential market for or value of the copyrighted work.

Public schools also benefit from three exemptions under the copyright law: face-to-face teaching at nonprofit educational institutions, educational broadcasting, and not-for-profit performances. In the first exception, instructors may generally read, perform, or display copyrighted material in a face-to-face address. Instructional broadcasting allows the performance of a non-dramatic literary or musical work for instructional purposes. Non-profit performances allow for the non-public performance of non-dramatic literary or musical works that are not for monetary gain.

Sexting

Even as we wrote this book, new issues related to technology have continued to surface. One such issue of particular concern involves what as been termed "sexting." The online encyclopedia *Wikipedia* describes sexting as follows: "Sexting (a [blend] of sex and texting) is the act of sending sexually explicit photos electronically, primarily between cell phones. It is practiced primarily by young adults, though it is known to occur amongst children as young as middle-school age." According to a survey conducted by the National Campaign to Support Teen and Unplanned Pregnancy, roughly 20 percent of teens admit to participating in sexting. In some cases, students participating in sexting have been charged with distribution of child pornography.

This recent phenomenon has caused a great deal of concern among school officials. It is important to remember the following when a student is suspected of sexting or possessing pornographic images:

Unless a student voluntarily consents to a search, school officials must have reasonable suspicion before searching a student's cell phone or camera for evidence of sexting.

Every effort should be made to assure that evidence of sexting is viewed only by an administrator who is of the same sex as the student appearing in the pictures.

School officials should carefully document all evidence, but should not keep copies of the actual images.

School officials are encouraged to call the parents of students who are distributing the pictures and the parents of students who are the subject of the pictures. However, privacy laws prevent school officials from discussing with a student's parents the names of other students who are involved with the situation.

As sexting could amount to child pornography and a violation of criminal law, the pictures should be turned over to police.

Conclusion

It is our hope that the above chapter is helpful in communicating to school officials some of the most important areas of schoolhouse technology. Please note that the above material primarily takes into account federal law and national trends. Your specific state may have additional laws or regulations that must be considered. Additionally, it is important to consult with your school attorney or legal advisor before taking final action with respect to any policy or practice within your school district.

Case Study #15: The Agnostic Superintendent and the Bible Bowl

South Elementary School District is a public school district located in Texas. Recently the school district added a "community events" section to its website where "any community organization can promote its upcoming events." Antonio Hughes, a died-in-the-wool agnostic and the district's superintendent, is in charge of monitoring the community events section of the website and removing any content that is inappropriate or does not meet the district's usage criteria. Recently, a local church posted to the community events section of the website, an advertisement for its upcoming "Bible Bowl," a Jeopardy-like competition for students to show their knowledge of the Old and New Testaments. Superintendent Hughes, believing that the church's use of the school district's website violated notions of separation of church and state, removed the church's post.

Legal Perspective:

Before delving into this scenario, it is necessary to provide a little background on public use of school district property in general. A school district may open up some aspect of itself to public use. For example, a school district could decide to allow community groups to use the school gymnasium on weekends, or the district could choose to send home advertisements for community events in student backpacks. School districts do have some discretion on how far to open the door to nonschool events and information sharing, but once the door is opened to one group, all similarly situated groups generally must be treated in the same manner.

The courts have placed access to school district property into three distinct categories, as follows:

Nonpublic (Closed) Forum: This is where a unit of government (including a school district) completely closes or limits the use of its property for the government's purpose. Here, the government may reserve the forum only for its intended purposes. For example, in *Perry Education Association v. Perry Local Educators' Association*, the United States Supreme Court held that union rivals could not use the school mail system, which had been reserved for school district business only. In this situation, the school district had "closed" the district's mail system, thus allowing it to only be used for school district-related information.

Limited (Designated) Public Forum: Here, the government has opened some aspect of itself for use for public use or expressive activity. The government can only impose reasonable, content-neutral time, place, and manner restrictions, so long as the restrictions are necessary and narrowly tailored to serve a compelling state interest. The government can generally close the forum at any time, but while the forum is open for some limited purpose, all similarly situated groups must be treated in the same manner. For example, a school district could decide to allow community groups to use its auditorium for a fee. All groups that pay the fee and follow the rules must be allowed equal use of the facility.

Open (Traditional) Public Forum: This is where people have the fullest First Amendment rights. Examples of open forums include parks and sidewalks, where anyone can erect their proverbial soapbox and espouse their viewpoints. Schools are generally not open public forums.

In returning to our case example, it is clear that the school district has decided to create a limited public forum as it applies to the use of the community events section of its website. As such, all community groups who follow the rules must be given equal access unless, of course, the school district has a compelling interest in disallowing a particular group to post information. Superintendent Agnostic has obviously determined that the church's posting of a religious event could be seen as the school district's endorsement of religion. He has therefore determined that there is a compelling interest to remove the content in question.

Fortunately, we can learn from what turns out to be an erroneous decision by Superintendent Agnostic. In fact, the United States Supreme Court addressed this exact question in 1993 in the case of *Lamb's Chapel v. Center Moriches School District.* In this case, Lamb's Chapel, a religious group, sought to use the school district's facilities to show a religious film on family values and child rearing. The school district had a policy of allowing community groups access to its facilities, but denied the request by Lamb's Chapel based on a New York state law preventing school districts from allowing religious groups access to school facilities after school hours for religious activities.

The Supreme Court, in a 9 to 0 opinion, overturned the decision of the lower courts, holding that the school district's decision to disallow the Chapel's use of school facilities amounted to viewpoint discrimination. The Court affirmed that once a school district opens its doors for public access it cannot selectively determine which viewpoints are acceptable and which are not. The Court further noted that there was effectively no issue regarding separation of church and state because the school district took no part in selecting the content of the films, nor were the films school-sponsored.

The *Lamb's Chapel* case is substantially similar to our case scenario. In both cases, the school district created a limited public forum. Likewise, in both cases the school district cannot engage in viewpoint discrimination. All parties that follow the rules must be treated the same, no matter what their message. Therefore, the superintendent's actions to remove the Bible Bowl information from the school district's website amounts to viewpoint discrimination and is not proper.

Two last points are important to make. First, it should be understood that once a school district creates a limited public forum, that forum need not be opened permanently. A school district can close the forum at any point, thereby effectively eliminating all public participation. Second, in creating a limited public forum, a school district can also decide how far to open the door. For example, in this case, the school district could limit the community events section of its website for only school-affiliated groups to post their announcements and events.

Administrative Perspective:

Thanks, Brian. However, I must admit you sound more like a law professor than my friendly lawyer in this case. "Limited public forum," "school-alleviated groups," and "compelling state interest" are terms I must admit are a bit unclear to my practicality-based cranial capacity. What is clear, at least to me, is your bottom line advice: open it up for everyone (with reasonable rules), or close it for everyone.

So, if Superintendent Hughes doesn't like having a preacher advertising for a night of Bible trivia on the school's "community event" web bulletin board, he better go to the board of education with a new policy, and it better be in accordance with the court rulings And, before he deletes, folds, staples, or mutilates the content on the website, he should place a friendly call to Larry the Lawyer and get some down-home advice on administering the existing policy and maybe a few examples of alternate policies for consideration. Too many of us in administration think we understand the separation of church and school (which we really don't) along with our supreme right to decide what can be published, who can rent, and what groups can have free access to our grounds and facilities. Each of these topics can be just too confusing and conflicting to be easily understood. And, we don't want to be wrong in our decisions, so just call Larry. You won't be the first principal or superintendent to make the call, nor the last, and Larry can probably give you quick advice over the phone. In this case, he would say to Antonio, don't mess with their posting unless it violates some of your established (and posted) rules, such as no profanity, no solicitation, no solicitation for profit-making events, no messages over 500 words, etc. Does this mean the church *and* the atheists are able to post messages? Yep, they can as long as they follow the rules.

So, if you don't want to deal with controversial groups, organizations, or messages, don't offer a community blackboard on your website.

This case story reminds me of a similar one that I actually experienced. Many years ago I inherited a school that allowed a group of folks to come into the building on an approved day to provide Bibles to any student in the fifth grade. They did not preach; they just said they had Bibles to give away and any student could have one. As school dismissed, they stood outside the classroom door and offered a Bible to every student who walked out. This event had been allowed for years and years.

The second year that I was the administrator in the district a parent came to my office and said she wanted to distribute a copy of a religious book to every student in the sixth grade. I asked her why she wanted to do this, and she said it was because the district allowed the Bible to be distributed, so she should be allowed to distribute the accepted book from her faith. I asked her if she approved of the Bible distribution, and she said no, she did not, even though she admitted it probably was the book of preference for almost all of the students in the community. I thanked her for coming in and told her that her request would be considered and that the existing policy would be reviewed. I promised to get back to her as soon as possible.

I had read the policy manual, all school handbooks, and everything the district had approved with rules and regulations. There was no policy written to permit the distribution of Bibles or any other materials in the school. As far as anyone could remember, this was established years ago and became a practice by precedence. No one could tell me when or how it started.

At the next meeting of the board of education, in open session, under the agenda item of "practice of distribution of reading materials," I shared the situation with the board with the recommendation that we discontinue the practice of allowing the Bibles to be distributed at the school and that we consider a formal policy that clarified what types of materials could be distributed at or via the school. The board agreed to discontinue the Bible distribution, and I was directed to review policies presented by either the school's law firm or the state's association for school boards. A few months later we adopted a formal policy which eliminated distribution of materials that were not provided by the school.

By the way, following that board meeting, I called the parent and told her what we had decided. She made it clear that was her intent, as if I didn't know that already. As Brian indicated earlier, you have to choose—everyone or no one. We chose no one.

This is not a tough topic, but sometimes it becomes a cloudy one when we forget that we are not the judge and jury for all decisions. While I would be repulsed to allow certain groups any opportunity to share their message through our school network, if I was eager to allow other organizations (like the Scouts, 4H, etc.) that same right, I would have to take the vinegar with the sugar. And so be it.

"If you laid all our laws end to end, there would be no end."

Mark Twain

Chapter Twelve

Parting Thoughts: There is no "Last Chapter" Chapter

Jim Burgett and Brian D. Schwartz

Introduction

This last chapter is the end, but it certainly isn't the end of the topic. Why? There is no end to the legal issues, situations, interpretations, negotiations, decisions, and actions taken by anyone and everyone in a school system, or for that matter, anywhere anytime. This is a crazy world where people do unexpected things for strange reasons. Thus, we always need to be as alert as possible and one step ahead of the push.

Administrators and board members need to continually learn and understand the changing laws and expectations of society, so they can develop and implement policy that allows staff to work, grow, and hopefully remain passionate about making a difference for kids. Not an easy task, but a necessary one.

Parents and teachers need to stay on top of their game to protect, teach, and move kids from point A to point B safely and sanely.

Kids? Well, the truth is that kids will adapt to the changes better than any of us, but still need reminders and nudges to keep them on the right path. And with all of the talk of legality and practicality, we still need to provide morality and compassion.

So, as we try to wrap up what we hope has been both an enjoyable and educational experience for you, the reader, we both want to share a few parting thoughts that also might be of help as you search for that Middle Ground in education. Here are some final thoughts. These aren't case studies, rather suggestions that we hope might help make your task a bit easier.

Jim's Final Thoughts: Keeping Brian in the Office

This is a practical suggestion for anyone who has faced the proverbial threat, "I'm going to call my lawyer!" For instance, you sit across a table from a pair of upset parents who feel that their daughter has been unfairly disciplined. In the middle of the conversation, they get frustrated, usually due to the fact that they aren't getting their way or because they truly know their daughter was wrong but still feel a need to defend her, or possibly because they really do believe the punishment doesn't fit the crime, at least for their child. So, when the frustration hits the boiling point, one parent announces, loudly and emphatically, "Enough of this, I'm calling my lawyer to make you people wake up and do what is right!"

I know that if you tweak the above circumstances, change the dialogue, and alter some of the parameters, you might easily morph the situation into one that you have actually experienced. When I provide training to administrators, board members, and teachers, I often ask how many have been threatened by the "call my lawyer" tactic? The vast majority raise their hands. By that number of hands, it's clear they are telling me that this lame tactic is overused. Unfortunately, some of the responders also tell me this type of "threat" occasionally works. Sometimes educators fold their hands when the lawyer card is played and give in to the demands on the table.

I want to share a response that works almost all the time. It's valid, honest, appropriate, and focused.

This proposed activity does require some advanced preparation and maybe a bit of practice. First, you need to know who your school counsel is—better yet, the name of not just the firm but also of a specific attorney who has represented the district. Then you need to obtain a small quantity of their business cards and have them where they are easily located. I kept my bundle in my top desk drawer. And finally, script carefully your response and memorize it. Why? You want to make sure you will remain cool and collected, and if ever questioned, you can pull out a copy of what you said or the script you generally follow.

Let me share how this works with an actual example.

Mr. and Mrs. White have come in to complain that their son Willy has been unfairly given a three-day in-school suspension for smoking in his car in the school parking lot, just as he was leaving on a Friday afternoon. The school's security officer caught him, called over the teacher on duty, and Willy was given a written notice to meet with the principal first thing on Monday morning. The principal met with Willy as scheduled, called the parents, and followed every step in the handbook with perfection. The parents came in and emphatically shared their opinion that when Willy is in his car, heading home, the rules of the school don't apply. His car is not the school, it is his space, and the school has no jurisdiction. Mr. White states he is a union worker and has strong feelings about personal rights and he is not about to cave in to the "stupid, petty, out-of-touch school rules." He clearly states that if Willy is old enough to drive, he is old enough to smoke, and his car is his personal space. It's like smoking at home, and the school "sure as hell doesn't rule in my home!" Period.

The principal reminds the Whites that they, and Willy, signed an agreement to follow the school policies when they returned their signed school handbook review form at enrollment. Mr. White blows it off, gets more agitated, and plays the lawyer card by saying "Enough of this bull sh__! My son has rights, and he is protected by the Constitution of the United States over and above some petty little book of rules by any high school. We're gonna contact our attorney, and you will see who is right."

Can't you just visualize this scenario?

The principal sits back, waits until Mr. White is done, and just before the mom and dad start to get up, he says the following, based on his script:

"Before you leave, let me tell you that indeed you have a right to involve an attorney, and we respect that right."

[This is when you open the drawer, pull out a card, and I suggest you circle the name of one of the attorneys on the card or write the name of an attorney on the back if it is a corporate card.]

"I'm sure you understand how lawyers work, but I am obligated to share with you our position regarding your right to involve your attorney. As you probably imagine, the district is represented by counsel, and we have been advised by our lawyers to give you their information so that your attorney can call our attorney directly."

"Once you have made the decision to involve your lawyer, a few things must be understood. Your lawyer, as well as ours, will advise you to discontinue conversations with the school. All future conversations will be conducted between the law firms. So, Mr. and Mrs. White, I cannot talk about Willy's situation with you until given that directive by our attorney. For that reason, the actions we have taken remain in place."

[You hand them the card and review the names and contact information on the card.]

"This information is for your attorney. Our lawyers will only talk to your counsel from this point."

"One final comment about this process, you are responsible for all expenses related to your attorney, and, of course, your taxes will pay for ours." (Don't smile during any of this!)

"Thank you for your time. I will call our attorney in a few minutes to advise him of the pending call from your counsel."

[You politely get up and help facilitate a professional ending to the conversation.]

End of the script.

Here is what usually happens. Either right there, or shortly after the Whites get home, they will indicate their desire to continue the discussion and not contact the attorney. Before you agree to do this, I suggest you remind them that they have already shared a desire to turn this issue over to legal counsel, which is their right, and you need to know that they have not engaged an attorney as they had indicated. If they have, you cannot, and will not, be able to resume discussion of the issue —per the directive by your legal counsel. You also need to remind them (if they indeed did leave the building before calling you back) that you have initiated contact with your attorney.

Why do this? The reasons are simple. Most issues are cookie-cutter situations where you have followed the law; thus, the discipline or actions are appropriate. In those instances where flexibility is acceptable, most administrators will bend and carry on reasonable negotiations; thus, attorney involvement is not needed. Again, in most situations, involving an attorney is a threat that adults feel will cause school officials to shrink and cower. Not so, if you are prepared. *If you are confident with your actions*, then answer their attorney card with your "real" card and go from there. If you feel an attorney will find a hole in your case (failure to follow the policy, over-reaction, prejudice to the student or family, etc.), then talk it through and find a reasonable solution. If you are wrong, you don't want an attorney involved!

Attorneys are wonderful people who help and guide us. We couldn't run a successful operation without them. However, if you can settle any issue on your own, without their direct involvement, it will usually take less time, cost far less money, and be more efficient.

As Brian and I wrote this book, we had many conversations about the challenges in education and how things really have become more complicated over the years and how there is always a new issue to contend with. We could list dozens of examples, but a few that have changed the way we operate over the past decade or so include Columbine, September 11, NCLB, the recession, and teaching standards. Adding to the mix of everyday challenges are technology, pornography, and the accessibility of illegal substances. Like I said, we could go on and on…

Well, Brian and I hoped that this book would help educators become better able to deal with these issues and others, but also better able to be *proactive rather than reactive*. In truth, we feel that if educators can anticipate problems, then maybe they can establish systems that prevent them. A simple analogy would be the uneven sidewalk. It doesn't take a rocket scientist to determine that if a sidewalk has fallen or lifted a couple of inches where it should be level, someone will undoubtedly trip. It is, as they say, an accident waiting to happen. The administrator that sees this situation and doesn't fix it is just inviting disaster. The same is true everywhere you look in a school system. A teacher that blows a gasket now and then may eventually cause irreversible harm if the behavior is not addressed. Need I go on? The proactive educator is far more productive than the reactive one.

The Link

Thus, I want to share a concept I call LINK. It is a process that hopefully allows a student to grow and mature with a minimum of issues. It works on the same principle as the IEP (Individual Education Plan). Since the late 1970's IEP's have been developed for special education students based on individual needs and goals. The LINK concept is similar in nature. It is simply a one-on-one opportunity for a student to have an advocate who will help him or her stay on the right track, find success, and avoid problems.

Here's how it works. Every certified and licensed staff member (people trained and legally able to work with students) becomes a LINK. Each LINK has a number of students that they take responsibility for. The LINKs don't discipline, and they don't teach; they just assist.

Now here is something almost unheard of in education—LINK is not an acronym! It means what it says: to link. Simply, the LINK is the student's connection with the world. The concept is as simple as the implementation. But, like all programs, it is only as successful as the people involved and their passion to make it work. Getting staff to understand, accept, and become productive LINKS takes some time, effort, and passion.

What are the details? How can it be initiated? What grade levels are best suited? What does a LINK do? Is money involved? These are typical questions, so let's try to answer them all with a few comments and an example.

LINK works best when students arrive at that time of their educational career when they leave the self-contained classroom. Up to this point, they had a teacher who was predominately assigned to them most of the day and in most traditional settings was the person "in charge" of watching out for the student's growth and welfare. In other words, the self-contained teacher was the LINK. So I would suggest that the middle school, junior high, or high school environment is probably the most natural setting to introduce the LINK concept.

Let's see the details through an example. Assume that we work at Montana Middle School. There are 450 students in this school in grades six, seven, and eight. If you count up all the possible LINKS (teachers, administrators, counselors, social workers, etc. that work full-time at the school), the number is 25. Now, if you divide the student body by eligible staff members, in comes to 18 students per LINK. (All students are included: regular education, special education, and gifted education.)

I like to suggest that each LINK be responsible for an equal number of students in each grade. For this situation that would mean each LINK would have approximately six sixth graders, six seventh graders, and six eighth graders. The rationale for dividing them this way is that a LINK can keep the same student throughout the student's three years at Montana Middle School.

When the program is first established, a draft system like they use in sports is used to select the students. I suggest that an entire list of students is made available to each of the 25 LINKS, and the staff members select students that they would like to work with, based on whatever reasons they feel are important. They submit their requests to a coordinator, who works with a master list and tries to fulfill as many requests as possible. The specific student requests are assigned during this first round. Staff members are also given the opportunity to request certain categories of students, such as "preference for special education students," "preference for athletes," or "preference for kids with some discipline history." Every district "customizes" this part of the process to meet its situation.

When the first round of assignments is made, a list of all students and their LINKs is shared with each staff member. A few days are allowed for "trading" to take place if someone gets a student they don't feel is best placed and seeks a trade for another student. This sometimes happens at a meeting of all the LINKS or over a short period of time. After the trading period is over, the lists are resubmitted, reviewed, and a final list is published. This process only happens when the program is first initiated. After that, at the beginning of each new school year, the incoming students are assigned to replace the "graduating" eighth graders, with the option that any LINK can request one of the sixth graders prior to the assignments. Again, a trading period takes place before the list is finalized.

Once the list is in place, the LINKS are asked to make contact with each of their students, in any way they deem appropriate, but not in a group setting. LINK students are not a team, and this is not a group activity. This is an opportunity for a staff member to LINK to a student, one-on-one, to facilitate success. Many begin the process with a note home, introducing themselves to the student and family, before school begins. Many call or email the student and try to make an appointment or time for a quick hello.

When the program is in place, it becomes a maintenance project, with the goal to maintain contact with the student. Notes, emails, calls, visits, appointments, etc. usually work. In most school settings, the LINK will see the student during the day or quickly discovers that he/she can be in connect before school, during a lunch hour, between classes, or at various times. It isn't as difficult to keep in contact as it might seem, and many LINKS ask the student to drop by once a week or so to keep in touch.

What does a LINK do? This is the beauty of the program, and some creativity makes it work really well. I have known schools that put the LINK's name in the same database with the students, and thus when a student is listed on the honor roll or on the D/F list or for some award, the LINK's name [or initials) is also automatically listed. When reports come out, it is easy to scan the list to find your student, or the list might be tied to an email notice so that the LINK actually receives an email notification when some award or notice is given. If a student is disciplined, the LINK is notified. If a student's parents come in, or some issue happens that can be appropriately shared with the LINK, he/she is notified. The LINK then goes into action with congratulations, words of encouragement, offering academic assistance, or conversations of motivation or support. Remember, the LINK does not discipline. The LINK encourages, offers help, and/or becomes an avenue for behavioral change or assistance. The goal of the LINK is to develop a meaningful relationship with the student.

An active LINK will tune in on the student's birthday, team membership, academic struggles, awards, and needs. All it takes for most students is an occasional note, high five, comment, or positive remark. For the ones that struggle, it might take some additional "linking" with appropriate resources. For example, I am a math teacher, and Benny Terwilliger is in my class and really, really struggling, including the absence of homework. I have talked to Benny with no success. I may very well email or talk to his LINK about the situation. The LINK may contact Benny, ask him how math is going, find out about the struggles, and actually discover what and why he is struggling. The LINK may suggest a meeting with the teacher and may even offer to sit in on it or may suggest another student as a mentor or even offer to have Benny come in after school and do his homework in the LINK's room.

If another teacher went to the LINK and said there has been a real change in Benny's behavior and outlook, and he simply doesn't seem to care about his work, the LINK may contact Benny and ask him if everything is okay. Since the LINK is not a threat or seen as a disciplinarian (but more as a caring adult, or "life coach"), Benny may open up and then the LINK might be able to connect Benny with a counselor or at least make appropriate suggestions.

Here is what LINK members aren't: social workers, counselors, deans of discipline, or administrators. Even when they might, in fact, have positions with similar titles or responsibilities (by their license and/or job assignments), they are not to exercise that role when serving as a LINK member. They are to be a caring adult. Not necessarily a "buddy," but someone the student trusts and feels comfortable talking with.

Does it always work? Does anything always work? The answer is, of course, no. Some staff members won't be the best LINKS because they won't make or take the time. Yet, when the system gains steam and people become passionate about it, the entire school climate changes, and kids succeed at record levels. Even when some LINKS are spelled DUDS, the ones who do their job as well as they can do make the difference, and, hopefully, when the DUDS see the effects of the real LINKS, they too can be morphed into agents of productivity.

What do you do if a LINK refuses to participate or thinks that this added role requires added pay, a kind of stipend for the time and effort? When that type of mentality exists, I suggest that the staff hasn't embraced the concepts of the program. It's not a paid assignment; it's what teachers do and what educating is all about—helping students find success. If teachers and/or staff members won't take the time or don't have the interest to embrace something this simple and basic, something that literally leaves the time commitment up to them, then I suggest the attitudes and compassion of the school as a unit need to be reviewed and altered.

How can you get a LINK program to grow in enthusiasm? Simple, you ask the successful LINKS to share their stories, how they manage their time, what they do to make it work, and generally brainstorm—all done during regular meetings, without calling special "LINK" meetings. I have even seen a LINK LETTER that was developed to share ideas and concepts between the LINKS, without naming students, of course.

And finally, why LINK? By interceding in the needs, successes, and challenges of students, you encourage positive behavior, build support, reduce stress, help eliminate discouragement and failure, and—one student at a time—you make a difference. And with enthusiastic leadership, the LINK program works and thrives, and the LINK grows along with the success of each student.

One more thing. I often discuss with educators what I call the 15% factor. I maintain that in most schools you can identify the students who cause the most trouble, take the most time, and do the least amount of work. It usually is a small percentage of the total enrollment. I have found it to average between 10 and 20 percent of the student body. It varies by school and community, but 15% is a good "average" number.

So, if we can substantially alter the attitudes and behavior of 15% of the student population, we can dramatically change the entire school climate. The LINK program fits right into this concept. If each LINK were to identify the most challenging three students of his/her group, and to effectively make a difference in their performance or attitudes, the program would dramatically improve 18% of the student body—the group that most needs the help and encouragement. If it took a couple of years to accomplish this goal, it would be worth the time and effort, and from that point, you just watch the entire system get better and do more. This proactive process really works!

Brian's Final Thoughts: Keeping Jim out of the ER

Well done, Jim. I hope it has come across in this book that Jim and I are very passionate about the fact that Middle Ground *can* be found. Your jobs are stressful enough as it is, and it is our hope that some of the thoughts and ideas that we have discussed in this book will assist you in effectively dealing with students, parents, the public, and each other.

As Jim has noted, we certainly have not covered every possible situation that can come up in education. And I am sure that in the time it takes for this book to be published, there will be new "situations" that will challenge our collective patience and sanity. However, no matter what the circumstances entail, it really all comes down to this:

- Know the law.
- Build relationships.
- Work through struggles together in an effort to find a solution that works for everyone involved.

Jim and I have been doing this long enough that we know that Middle Ground can be found through this simple formula. Sometimes it takes a great deal of time, understanding, and compassion, but our experiences firmly lead us to believe that it works!

In his final comments, Jim states that lawyers have a necessary place in the field of education. However, the most important job, by far, is done by teachers, administrators, and school board members. Lawyers generally advise and counsel, but it is up to educators to take these recommendations and successfully implement them.

My wife Jennifer is the assistant principal at a nearby elementary school, so last week when I called her, I could tell by the background noise that there was a great deal of commotion at the school. I was politely informed by the secretary that "Jennifer cannot come to the phone right now. She is chasing a naked boy." That night, I got some more details of the incident. As it turned out, an eight-year-old student had decided to strip off all of his clothing and run screaming through the school, and it was Jennifer's job to catch him.

Clearly, a call to the lawyer in this situation would have been of little help. Although my job is no picnic, on my worst day as a lawyer, I have never had to chase a naked child through the halls—nor do I ever intend to!

I am sure that when my wife reads this book, she will be absolutely mortified that I have shared this story with you. However, I can think of no better example to make this point: an educator's job is more demanding and stressful than those of most other occupations. I am thankful that there are people like you—the reader—who have chosen to take on the tremendous responsibility to educate America's future, despite the imperfect system in which you must accomplish this task.

On behalf of both Jim and me, we hope you have enjoyed reading this book as much as we have enjoyed writing it for you. We hope that it will help to make your job a little easier as you search for Middle Ground.

Plus two bonus case studies...

These involve topics and information earlier shared and are included to help reinforce the need to seek Middle Ground that includes both legal and practical advice.

Case Study #16: What is Popping?

Mary Popping is a freshman girl who moved into the district in October. She is slowly making some friends and seems to fit in well. On the first day back to school after winter vacation, one of Mary's new friends notices that Mary is slurring her words and has popped something into her mouth while at her locker. The friend is concerned about Mary and reports this series of events to Mary's physics teacher at the beginning of the first hour.

Administrative Perspective:

Not much to go on here, but that is the case with a lot of situations, so let's talk some strategy.

There are three players in this case study to begin with: Mary, the new student, Mary's friend (Friend), and the physics teacher (PT). Right off the bat, there is a decision to be made by the teacher that will reflect the level of training he has received concerning situations like this and the level of common sense the teacher displays. The teacher's actions will, to some degree, reflect the administration's ability to successfully do three things: hire a good staff, train that staff appropriately, and retain and retrain that staff as needed. This is huge. The teacher could, in only a few minutes, cause great problems for the district, for Mary, and for the community if he handles this situation inappropriately:

- The teacher could go directly to Mary's locker and conduct an illegal search, violating Mary's rights and maybe the district's policies.

- The teacher could call Mary over and accuse her of something that could damage her relationship with her peers and establish a cloud over her character possibly forever.

- The teacher could ignore the situation and it could become life threatening or dangerous to others.

Is the teacher important at this stage in the case study? Do bears like to hibernate? Are you kidding?

So let's assume we have an intelligent, thoughtful, and compassionate teacher. PT has been trained to deal with this situation. He and the staff ran through a few "mock" situations at faculty meetings, and he attended some training on search procedures and student intervention at institutes. Right now PT is glad about the training. PT recognizes the complexity of the situation, the ramifications of handling it right, and the necessity of action.

Remember, PT learns of the concern at the beginning of the first hour, and he needs to share the issue with an appropriate administrator.

Let's run through three possibilities that might cover the most reasonable options:

First possibility: Let's assume PT works in a moderate to large high school that has more than one layer of administration (deans, assistant principals, and principal). In this case, PT needs to know to whom he reports this situation. That alone requires an understanding of the administrative structure and who is responsible for what. There is a safety net here, however. If he reports this to the wrong person, they should know to whom to transfer the question. In either case, PT is covered.

Second possibility: Let's assume this is a small school and/or small district and PT has only the principal between him and the superintendent. PT goes to the principal with the situation; if successful, PT is covered. If not, PT takes the situation to the superintendent. In this case, PT should be sure that the principal has some form of notice that PT delivered a serious situation to the superintendent in his/her absence.

Third (and scariest) possibility: No matter what the size of the school, let's assume no administrator is present to handle the issue. PT is alone. Does this happen very often? Sure it does, and it only reinforces the value and need of good administration. But, for a moment, let's assume PT is in charge of the situation. Certainly something needs to be done, and it needs to be done now.

So the first thing PT needs to do is involve the fourth character in this situation, preferably the administrator who is responsible for student behavior and welfare. If PT cannot locate this person, the goal is still to involve another qualified staff member. I would first make an immediate effort to contact an administrator by phone for directions. If this fails, then consider a counselor, social worker, nurse, or other student assistance professional who can help assess the student's health or situation.

Logistically, there are a few things PT must do to initiate any action. A lot of what takes place depends on the structure and opportunities of the facility. Remember, from what we know, the friend notified PT at the beginning of first hour; thus, we are to assume PT has a class to teach. Teachers are told, time after time, not to leave a class unattended. I reminded my staff, persistently, that when they walked out of the room and left their class with no adult supervision, they were to visualize a big "L" in their personal view finder until they returned. That "L" stood for LIABLE. Whatever happened in their absence was their responsibility. I often shared war stories, some from personal experience as a teacher and administrator and some from the RSS (Really Scary Stuff) file. Brian has a huge RSS file he refers to almost every day!

Hopefully, this school has been proactive and has installed and maintains a two-way communication system from every room to the office, and maybe to the outside world. Let's assume they do. PT picks up the phone and gives a silent code to the office. PT may say I need Red Service. The operator/receptionist/office secretary knows that Red Service means to send an administrator to my room as soon as possible or send an adult to cover my class. I need to see an administrator now. There is a short list of coded messages that PT selects from. For instance, Blue Service might mean I have an issue that requires face-to-face communication, but is not an immediate need. Green Service may mean I have an emergency—send two or more people to my room ASAP. The neat thing about this type of code is that the teacher can call and request it quietly enough that no one is alerted, but the office is aware that a situation needs assistance. If there is no phone or intercom, PT may need to step out in the hall to notify the next teacher that he/she needs to cover both classes or get an adult humanoid from some location to cover.

The success of any solution is indeed in the details, and as you will read throughout this book, we like to cover the "what-ifs" for a teacher or administrator so that when a crisis happens, the bases can be covered quickly, legally, and appropriately. Things like communication systems are far more complicated that just installing a phone; to be effective they must also include training and procedures.

Let's return to the case study. Let's assume that PT has either contacted an administrator to take over or has been able to find someone to cover the physics class and has a partner to help with the next steps. Or that PT was able to get a guidance counselor to help.

If an administrator is involved, he/she will get the transfer of information from PT and take over. PT goes back to teaching and follows the code of ethical behavior by not sharing anything with anyone at this time. Gossip or innuendo can do drastic harm to the parties involved. It is human nature to want to the source of juicy information, so it takes conscious effort to be professional. Mary may be sick, may be taking cold medicine, may be falsely accused by her "friend" who doesn't like the fact that Mary is cuter and draws more attention from the boys than she does. Mary may be drunk or on drugs and runs a drug dealership from her locker. The truth is YOU DON'T KNOW, and thus you SHOULDN'T SPECULATE. In professional terms, PT's job right now is to zip it shut.

If an administrator is not involved and direction from one cannot be acquired—meaning that efforts to bring a district administrator to the high school have also failed—then PT should quickly write a plan of attack with the other staff member (we agreed it was a counselor) and then proceed as they agree is prudent. Let's say they agree on the following steps and documented them before they took action: (1) make sure all classes and obligations are covered by adult supervision; (2) interview Mary to do an assessment on her physical and mental condition; (3) depending the outcome of the interview, if Mary appears ill or appears to have been consuming alcohol or drugs, contact her parents and ask them to come in ASAP; (4) if no parent is available, determine from the list of emergency contacts if a parent can be reached, trying not to involve the emergency contact unless absolutely necessary; (5) not conduct a locker search without administrative assistance and/or direction; (6) if needed, bring in the Friend for a follow-up interview while all facts remain fresh; and (7) if Mary has been drinking or using drugs and the parents come in, inform them that the administration will be contacting them and will most likely do a follow-up with the police.

The goal here is to assure Mary's welfare and get her in a safe place. Hopefully, the family will assist and work with the school. In most cases they do. In some cases, involving the family just adds more fuel to the fire, but so be it. You take the problem one step at a time.

If an administrator was involved, he/she would have the experience and know the next steps to take, if necessary. If Mary admits that she and two other kids drank some wine in the car on the way to school, you now have other kids to interview, and the situation just got bigger and more difficult. If Mary tells you she has a gulp or two of vodka every morning and has for the past year, you have a family/student issue to work through. The school can be a savior to this student and family with assistance and intervention. This may be the best day in Mary's new life now that help can be injected into her existence. Mary doesn't need to be punished; she needs help.

If Mary is obviously intoxicated and offers no help, the administrator now needs to review the locker search policy, put on his/her investigator uniform, and start the long and arduous process of fact gathering. Mary isn't cooperating, and this may be a problem that involves more than just Mary. The first (and often most productive) search for facts comes from the school, not the police. At some point, the school involves the police and even turns everything over to them, but most school folks know that *good administrators* know their students and school community far better than any other agency. There are so many "what-ifs" in this case study that I could outline a dozen or so possible outcomes. Let me end with the following summary statements and then let Brian give us his input:

- Teachers need to know how to process information in a timely, efficient, and compassionate manner.

- Teachers should not leave classes unattended if it can be avoided.

- Two-way communication systems are imperative for all areas within a school.

- Procedures for responding to teacher communications should be established and reviewed and followed.

- Student safety and welfare trump punishment and, in time, procedures.

- In the absence of set policy or procedure, plan and document all steps, taking complete notes for future reference.

- With respect to search processes, of a person or of property, follow established procedures. If those procedures do not exist, adopt a legally supported policy and train all those responsible for its implementation. There is no room for error with this issue.

- Before you involve the police or outside agencies, involve the parents, unless there is concern for safety.

- Remember, in all cases involving humans, gossip is dangerous and damaging. Use ethical and professional standards. Ask yourself this question, "If this was my child, how would I like this to be handled?"

OK, Brian, your turn…

Legal Perspective:

Thanks, Jim. This case study certainly illustrates how a situation can spiral out of control if it is not handled properly. You are certainly right when you indicate that in the world of teaching and administration, decisions need to be made both quickly and correctly, especially when it comes to students who are entrusted to your care. And you're right: lawyers, the news media, the general public, parents, and law enforcement will have the luxury of hindsight as "Monday morning quarterbacks" in analyzing the decisions that school leaders had only minutes—or even seconds—to make.

In this case, the advice you give is right on the mark. Let me direct my on-the-spot analysis to what happens when things are not handled in such a professional manner.

First, though, let me provide some general reassurances for teachers and administrators who take the time to act in the best interest of students.

As Jim notes, the safety of the student is the key factor in this situation. After the tragedy at Columbine High School and others like it nationwide, the judicial system has softened its approach in dealing with lawsuits against school districts and school employees who need to make quick decisions to protect students in their custody. Generally what we have seen is that courts are unlikely to impose significant liability in cases where administrators, teachers, and other school employees act in the best interest of kids.

For example, using a similar scenario to the one in this case study, suppose that you, as a teacher or administrator, are approached by a student who is crying uncontrollably and indicates that her friend needs help. When you get to the friend, she is lying on the floor and is having a seizure. You ask if anyone saw anything happen as you try to restrain the student to keep her from causing further injury to herself. From the crowd, you hear a voice indicate that the student in question ingested a large amount of drugs that morning. You grab the student's purse and empty in on the floor, but there are no drugs present. Another passing teacher yells to you that the student has a seizure disorder and that restraining the student could cause further damage. Fortunately, the student recovers quickly from the seizure, but in your efforts to help by restraining the student's movement, you have broken several of her ribs.

Although the above story may sound farfetched, it is similar to one that I dealt with as a rookie attorney. In the case I handled, the parents of the student who had the seizure sued the teacher and the school district. Specifically, the parents pursued three claims in their lawsuit: (1) the medical aid rendered by the teacher was unreasonable and caused the student's injuries, (2) emptying the student's purse on the floor amounted to an illegal search, and (3) the second teacher violated the student's privacy rights by disclosing in front of a large crowd that the student had a seizure disorder.

In this case, the school district and employees were absolved of all liability. As for the medical aid, the court found that the teacher was protected by a Good Samaritan-type statute and acted reasonably under the circumstances known to the teacher at the time. The court further found that the search of the student's purse was a "reasonable" response in an attempt to protect the student's well-being. Lastly, the court found that under federal law and the law of the state, a student's privacy can be breeched for emergency medical reasons.

In the above case, the good guys won and all ended well. The actions of all parties were deemed reasonable under the circumstances and were done in the best interest of protecting the student. Now, let us turn our attention again to Mary. As you will recall, Mary's friend indicated to a teacher that Mary was slurring her words and had popped something into her mouth while at her locker. The friend, claiming concern for Mary, reported the above events to Mary's first hour teacher.

As we discussed in Chapter One, teachers and administrators must act reasonably given their specialized training and the circumstances that presently exist. In this case, it is not reasonable for the first hour teacher to turn his back on the situation, figuring that "Mary looks fine." The teacher must, in accordance with the reasonableness standard, take actions to further assess the situation. This may involve talking to

Mary directly or immediately referring the matter to an administrator. Likewise, an administrator who is brought up to speed on the facts of this case will need to investigate the situation. Failure of the administrator to act because "Mary is a good girl and would never take drugs" or based on the perception that Mary looked okay is inherently unreasonable and could result in personal liability if anything happens to Mary.

One might be compelled to argue that anything that happens to Mary is her own fault, as she is the one who took the drugs and therefore caused the injuries to herself. This argument would fall on deaf ears if ever pursued in court. It is extremely important to remember that as teachers and administrators we assume a duty to protect students—all students—who are placed in our custody. Failure to act to protect a student, even in situations where the student's own actions are the initial cause of her injuries, is inherently unreasonable in the eyes of the law.

Jim also discusses the issue of confidentiality in his comments. Although confidentiality can be breeched in cases of an emergency, teachers and administrators must take great care to protect a student's privacy. When an emergency exists, school officials must be careful not to disclose more information than may be necessary to address the situation. Additionally, once the emergency has abated, all student privacy rights and constitutional rights must be protected in a follow-up investigation. Again, failure to follow proper procedures can result not only in a lawsuit, but personal liability as well!

Case Study #17: Potluck

South Elementary School has a yearly festival where students perform for parents, and then parents, students, and teachers enjoy a "potluck" style lunch. South is a school with a poverty level of 85%, and this is the only event of the year when teachers have a chance to interact with several of the parents. Recently, the school board has become concerned about the issue of food poisoning after several students in a neighboring district became sick after a similar type of event. The school board president has suggested canceling this event to avoid potential problems, including the possibility of a lawsuit.

Legal Perspective:

I have tried very hard throughout this book not to be the "bad guy" who puts an end to all the fun. This time I'm afraid that I am going to have to put on my mean lawyer hat. (I really do have a mean lawyer hat. It was a gift from Jim.) But before I give my advice—and it is going to be short and sweet—please keep in mind that my job is keep you legally safe, although even here, I think Jim and I are going to be able to find Middle Ground.

Here it goes. School districts have recently been forced to take somewhat drastic means to keep kids safe and healthy. There have been a number of cases where students and staff have become ill from unsanitary food preparation. This has led to restrictions on the types of food kids can bring to school to share with others. It has also led to restrictions on the types of foods that parents and students can bring to the type of school/community event that is discussed in the case scenario.

So, I understand the school board president's concern. However, the show must go on, so let's find Middle Ground!

To start, I like a policy stating that "all food brought into the school or to school events by parents and students must be purchased at a store, be individually wrapped, and not require refrigeration." This certainly is not a complete policy, but it gives you the idea of where I am coming from: food prepared in private homes, food that is not individually wrapped, and food that can spoil are not allowed. And please keep in mind that this policy is not intended to ruin the lunch. It is meant to keep the luncheon attendees healthy and assure that these types of events can continue in the future.

But let's explore a few more ways to comply with the above policy. First, the school could request that parents make a monetary contribution toward the purchase of food, and school employees could actually purchase the items. However, given South's poverty level, this may be impractical. Alternatively, parents could be given a list of items that they can purchase at the store that are acceptable, and the school district could appoint a staff member to examine the items as they are brought to the event. My last suggestion is for the school to seek community support and contributions to cover the costs of the event, although this again may not be entirely practical depending on the economic conditions of the local community.

I am really interested in hearing Jim's comments here. It's critical for this event to continue in order to provide an opportunity for parents and teachers to communicate with each other.

Administrative Perspective:

If indeed "necessity is the mother of invention," let's find a way to make this important foodfest happen!

It sounds like the entertainment festival at South Elementary School is an important and enjoyable event and that eating is a major part of the fun. But also that the rules of the old potluck have gone the way of Pac Man.

When the "food rules" came out several years ago, they first appeared as suggestions by health departments and then became legislation in many states. When that happened, I balked. What? No "candy" sales during noon hour to raise a little money for the PTA or cheerleaders or Science Club? No table with a display of soft, gooey, chocolate chip brownies, sugar cookies, or cream puffs? No homemade pie slices at the kids' carnival in March? No chili from Mrs. Petterson at the Halloween Hullaballoo? This is total nonsense! What have those blasphemous morons at the state capitol been smoking?

And then I thought about the annual Junior Prom dinner. This was an event held right before the Junior Prom dance and was a tradition at one of the high schools where I worked. The Senior Prom was the big one, held at a fancy place with all the extras, so they downplayed the details of Junior Prom. Suits, not tuxedos, nice dresses, not gowns that required a second mortgage, and a dinner at the school followed by a semi-fancy dance in the gym. The dinner was a gift from the parents of the juniors, and this was a long-standing school tradition. The parents would decorate the cafeteria, set the tables with nice ware, and have a family style dinner, where they served a couple of fancy meats or fish entrees, complete with salad, mashed potatoes, and veggies. Plus the much awaited table of delicious pies and cakes that the moms and grandmothers had prepared.

Many were specialties. I loved the pecan pie made by Grandma Rose. At this table, you didn't get the tiny little pieces served at weddings. These were humongous slices that every junior boy relished. It was a great meal—except for the potatoes.

You see, Mrs. Spudini (name changed to avoid a lawsuit) proudly brought a big steaming bowl of mashed potatoes to the event every year. The Spudinis graced the world with a number of offspring, so we were lucky to have her gifts for a long span of time. Even if she didn't have a junior, she would bring the potatoes. That's just the way she was.

A few of us in the system had the distinct experience of visiting the Spudini home. It was a two story house on a small farm outside of town. There's a lot of ways to describe homes—cottages, colonial, ranch, etc. The best word I can come up with is "dump." Several times I called upon the county health department to visit the Spudini home to assist with hygiene issues that the kids displayed and other things too gross to describe here. Once a plumber told me he was called to the house to repair the dishwasher. Seems Mrs. Spudini had run a cycle with some chickens as the only item in the washer. She had prepared the little creatures by cutting off their heads, hanging them on the clothesline to drain them, and then running them through the dishwasher to remove the feathers. Mrs. Spudini was creative beyond her time.

So it was known around the inner circle of the school to avoid the Spudini spuds at all cost. However, at times, the bowls of mashed potatoes were combined into one large pot, and the game was over—the Spudini gift was now communal. Yikes! So if you knew, you avoided the potatoes.

Did anyone get sick at the prom? Probably. Did we have a fatal attack from diseased tators? Not that I know of. Was the Spudini contribution lethal, or even inappropriate? Who knows? Was it worth the chance that someone might get sick? Of course not. But we also served desserts with peanut butter in them—who knew then?

So, today we dump the old traditions and replace them with government protection. We cover for the parent who cooks on the dirty countertop, who never sanitizes the sponge that sits on the sink, who uses old and spoiled products, who doesn't cook the brew long enough, or who fails to be safe and sanitary in a dozen other ways. Today we simply say—bring something prepared and sealed, with ingredients listed, by an organization that is approved and certified or have a meal catered by a company that is subject to health inspection. ***Take no chances; thus call no ambulances.*** Now that's another thing my grandmother would never say.

When I was a little boy, I used to stand in the front seat of my dad's Jeep Wagoneer and pretend to shoot passing cars with my Lone Ranger cap gun. When he bought a little Nash Metropolitan convertible, my friends and I would stand on the back seat, hold onto the rails on the sides, and pretend to be flying. We only did those things in town, on the back roads, but we did them, and it was fun. Today my dad would be serving 10-15 years for child cruelty, seat belt violation, and contributing to the delinquency of a minor. He might also serve time for buying a Nash. He also used to let me drive on the back alleys when I was 13, just for fun. And, boy, was it. And, sick as it was, we ate pies made from strangers at church. Come to think of it, we still do. And, I'm still alive, not a delinquent, and rather healthy for an old guy. But I think the rules in place today are valid and sane. A lot of kids avoid illness and accident by following the regulations we have adopted. Thus, food poisoning, accidental or on purpose, is avoided by simply using good common sense.

So I agree wholeheartedly with Brian. We aren't the bad guys here. Mrs. Spudini is. Finding Middle Ground in this case study is easy. Call together the committee of teachers and/or parents who plan and implement the festival and brainstorm options. Brian named a few of the obvious ones—bring packaged food, have the meal catered, collect money for the cost, find a sponsor to pick up or supplement the tab, or skip the meal and just have the entertainment. Or maybe have a hot dog roast with potato chips and canned baked beans, where everything is store purchased, wrapped, safe, and simple.

So here is a quick summary of this tale. Some rules are hard to swallow because they don't seem to make sense, but usually, and I really mean this, usually they are right. If you decide to follow them and move on, making them the "mother of invention," you will find ways to replace or improve old traditions with newer, safer ones. If you elect not to follow them, you face the opportunity to meet Brian, face-to-face, or one of his partners in legal justice, when you are called to come head to gavel with the definers of the "L" word, LIABILITY. So be a good camper; follow the rules.

And one more thing, if the Spudini family invites you to dinner, take them to Applebee's.

Case Study #18:
Raphael Gets Clipped ... or Does He?

Billy Zipperman is a minority student with a slight learning disability. He lives with his elderly grandmother, and no one at the school has ever met or is aware that a parent exists. Billy is in fifth grade and is an average student with no discipline record. Mr. Travis, the golden-haired sixth grade science teacher, hears a ruckus in the boys' bathroom and walks in on a loud argument between Billy and Rafael, an eighth grade boy. Mr. Travis hears Rafael address Billy with a racial slur and steps between the boys. Rafael immediately charges that Billy pulled a "blade" on him. Billy says he was using his fingernail clippers when Rafael came in the restroom and started the fight.

Administrative Perspective:

Jim gets the first shot on this one….

Rafael is an eighth grader. For the sake of conversation, let's say he is 13 years old. Billy is a fifth grader. Let's put him at 10. Having taught boys in this age range for many years, it is quite possible that Rafael is a foot taller and many pounds heavier than Billy. Not always, but it's probable. It is also quite possible that Billy and his nail clippers are about as scary as Donald Duck. Of course, there is the possibility that Billy gets enraged when called a name, and thus he could be quite a nuisance, maybe even dangerous with those old clippers of his.

There are a number of issues here to consider. As with every situation at the old schoolhouse, a good educator (teacher or administrator) will document the findings, do it promptly, and do it in detail. Remember the three D's they taught you in grad school: Document, document, and document.

So far, here is what we know:

- Mr. Travis heard what sounded like an argument in the restroom.
- No other students were mentioned as being present.

- Mr. Travis heard Rafael address Billy with a racial slur.
- Mr. Travis enters the restroom and steps between the boys.
- Rafael says Billy "pulled a blade" on him.
- Billy says he was using his fingernail clippers when Rafael came in and started the fight.
- There is no documentation of any physical contact between Billy and Rafael or any attack with those nasty clippers.

This type of situation is challenging for a number of reasons. First, and most important, there is the lack of supportive evidence. A lack of witnesses and cameras seldom helps to solve a problem. Second, there is the potential for something little to become huge or something huge to fall through the cracks. Third is the fact that situations like this can take a horrendous amount of time.

Do we need a lawyer or a course on constitutional law in the case of Billy and Rafael? Honestly, it all depends on how well the educators can get the boys to fess up, how reasonable the parents/guardians will be, and what kind of legal counsel the district has. Most lawyers are rational folks who work on a substantial foundation of common sense. They don't try to make a federal case out of a simple situation of two boys acting up. However, and there always is a "however" in life, some lawyers are hung up on rights and rules and forget about handshakes and rational parental involvement.

My first suggestion is that Mr. Travis takes the boys and the facts to Judy, the administrator, who hopefully knows the individuals. He should share exactly what he saw and heard. Then he should immediately write down his recollection of everything and everyone involved, giving Judy a copy. Dates, times, places, quotes, attitudes, and impressions should be carefully documented. Just like on TV. Mr. Travis should prepare for the federal grand jury while hoping for Judge Judy garnishing a successful resolution before the first commercial.

If I were Judy, I would hear all sides and then ask for a short recess. I would quickly review the records of both kids and the handbook and policy manual to see if nail clippers fall in the same category as a weapon or if they are permitted for such duties as trimming nails. If I am not sure about the rules or if past precedence might come into play, I would ask. I'd ask another administrator or ask an experienced teacher if all the administrators are still wet behind the ears. An alternate scenario would be to call the attorney. Why the reluctance in calling the attorney with this case? Because you just might be able to solve this one using tact, compassion, guilt, guidance, listening, and resolution skills, rather than involving case law and checklist consequences. The administrator also needs to understand the words that were used, their meanings as it relates to kids, as well as adults, and the posted rules for racial degradation.

Once the administrator gathers the facts of the case, checks the handbook procedures and school district policies, and investigates the law, she can begin the real task of finding a solution.

One small caveat exists in this case: Billy is a special education student. This means that Judy has to investigate Billy's IEP and past history. Does he have a behavior problem or history of violence, is his grandmother legally the person to contact, and a myriad of other details which should be evident in the records and from a quick conversation with Billy's teacher.

After doing this preliminary homework, I would call the legal parents or guardians and hope for the best. I would notify them of the situation and let them know that you will be talking to the boys to get both sides in a sincere effort to understand the conflict and, hopefully, resolve the case appropriately. God may shine on Judy by providing parents and guardians with faith in the school and a willingness to let Judy perform her magic. Let's make an assumption here. Let's assume that Judy was able to contact a managing "parent" for both of the boys and they agree to let Judy pursue her investigation while keeping them informed. This assumption presumes that neither parent, semi-parent, guardian, or stepparent went off the deep end, wanting the finger-clipper prosecuted for battery or the name-caller sent to juvyland. A personal note here: I have found that the majority of parents are reasonable and responsible and will work with any educator (teacher or administrator) if they trust him/her. Building that trust starts very early in the relationship between school and home and is key to providing a successful learning and growing experience.

Back to work. Judy begins the investigative process, something she has learned through experience and not in grad school. She talks to (not interrogates) both boys separately while keeping them isolated from others and each other. This is where a quiet study room or small office is not a luxury, but a necessity. It becomes a holding room for the boys. The process that seems to work is this: (1) both boys are taken to their lockers and allowed to get books (no phones or electronic devices), (2) individually they are given the opportunity to study or read while waiting, and (3) they are given a chance to calm down if needed.

They might even be offered water or soda while waiting. Why go through all this for two boys who were in a disturbance? It doesn't take a degree in psychology to know that the more calm and settled they become, the more rational they will act when questioned.

Judy seeks history as well as facts. Do they know each other? Is there a past problem? Is there a gang or prejudicial association involved? Have they been at each other before? Is there a problem with siblings or family members, neighborhoods, or units of association? Does Billy's special education needs or status play a role in this issue? The goal is to discover not only why this happened, but also if this is more than a one-time conflict.

Along with history come the facts of the situation. What was Billy doing with the clippers? Why was he in the restroom, who sent him, and at what time? The same questions need to be answered about Rafael. If Mr. Travis hasn't provided this information, Judy needs to get it.

There are so many ways this case can go, and all are important. Here is a short list of what Judy might consider:

- Is this situation a reflection of prejudice and/or racial problems in the school?
- Are the clippers really a source of protection or weaponry?
- Are there greater issues involved here?
- Was this an isolated case of inappropriate interaction between two boys, with no real "corporate" significance?
- Do we make a mountain out of this molehill, or is this already a mountain, of sorts?

Judy has a lot on her plate. Maybe the name Raphael used was not offensive to Billy. Maybe it has a whole different meaning to 10-13 year old boys than it does to adults. Maybe the name-calling wasn't even the big issue. Judy needs to find the answers to these questions as best she can, and quickly.

Another consideration is the clippers. Lots of schools have a descriptive list of weapons. Sometimes the actual length of the blade or instrument comes into play. Maybe these clippers didn't even have a file included. And maybe the intent of the clippers was not for personal hygiene, but, just as Raphael suspected, to be threatening or used to harm. I guess this brings into play the old question about what is a weapon. Personally, I think I can do a lot more harm to another person with a ballpoint pen or pencil, than I could with my nail clippers. I could also do a lot of harm with my comb, my iPod, or my shoe. So I guess the weapon element depends on the use and intent as much as the tool itself, assuming we aren't talking about "real" weapons like guns and hand grenades.

So where are we now? Judy has interviewed both boys and reviewed the documentation from Mr. Travis, the kids' school files, and existing policies and practices. She has successfully contacted a legal "parent" for each boy and now has to make a determination.

There are as many options as you can imagine in a case like this, but the important thing is that Judy is doing her job well. I'm sure Brian agrees that in most cases within a school the educator is the one-stop-shop for finding a successful resolution. The classroom teacher solves disputes daily, maybe even hourly. The administrator, who gets the bigger problems or problems that happen in the "school" arena rather than the classroom, may need a longer list of tools and more involvement. It all comes with the territory. So, in the case of Billy and Raphael, it can be complicated or simple.

This case might be solved by a handshake, an apology, and a short lecture on kindness and respect, followed up with the same report to both sets of parents and the teachers involved. And, hopefully, it will garnish some support at home. Or it might involve some sort of district/school discipline, maybe even a suspension, or, if a weapon is truly determined to have been used with the intent to harm, consideration of expulsion, or an IEP hearing/staffing/revision might even be considered. I certainly hope not. Suspension and expulsion to me have always been consequences that should be reserved for consideration only when other forms of discipline are exhausted or when safety is an issue.

Both of these boys have rights and should be afforded due process. Because Billy is a special education student, his list of rights and responsibilities is probably the longest anywhere in the world. Neither, however, has the right to disrupt the school operation or become a nuisance or threat to others. Neither has the right to call anyone derogatory names or put anyone in harm's way. Judy's job is to determine if either boy messed with the constitutional rights of the other or if either did something so horrendous as to put the school or its operation in peril.

I know how I want this to end. I want it to be two boys who got hot under the collar at each other for a minute, meant no significant harm to anyone, and realize, quickly, that they made a mistake. I want Judge Judy to diligently gather her information and make her decision based on good investigative work and research and to end this issue as a win-win-win. The first win is that the boys learn and gain control of their behavior and respect for others. The second win is that both parents use this issue to teach their kids and gain respect for Judy and the system. The third win is for Judy—another notch on her key ring of successful conflict resolutions and a shining example to others of good management skills, caring leadership, and protection of the rights and responsibilities of everyone.

Legal Perspective:

This is a very interesting scenario, and one where there is no good place to begin. I think that Jim makes an important point in that this is not necessarily a situation where the principal needs to start with a phone call to the school district's attorney. I must admit that a great deal of what Jim discusses is really outside the purview and expertise of an attorney. It is rather a matter of relationships and good old-fashioned common sense.

I must also admit that when I first read this case scenario, it appeared to be nothing more than a simple situation of two students arguing in a restroom. I initially thought: find the culprit, give him a detention, place a call to his parents, and move on to the next crisis. However, as I started to write, it became painfully evident how complex this situation actually is or might become.

After reading Jim's comments, perhaps what strikes me most about this scenario is that it requires the teacher and principal to incorporate a great number of the skills and concepts that we have already discussed in this book, mainly: keeping yourself legally safe (Chapter 1), student due process rights (Chapter 2), search and seizure (Chapter 3), student records and privacy (Chapter 6), and dealing with minority student populations (Chapter 10). It may also involve discipline for off-campus conduct, depending on where this situation originated (Chapter 4) and possibly dealing with difficult parents or guardians (Chapter 8).

This is a great deal to think and worry about for a "simple argument." All this while the principal is trying to deal with the other issues of running a school, not the least of which is trying to find time to focus on being the instructional leader!

It is first important that Teacher Travis use no more force than is reasonably necessary to take the students to the principal's office. Jim and I have both dealt with situations where teachers have incurred personal liability for using excessive force in dealing with students. It is certainly permissible to use more force where safety requires it, but in this situation—absent the students coming to blows—it is prudent for the teacher to only place his hands on the students to guide them to the principal's office. Ideally, of course, another responsible adult will be present to assist in this process in order to keep the students somewhat separated.

When the students are brought to Principal Judy, she should separate the boys and first deal with Billy to determine if the nail clippers pose any real safety risk. From a Fourth Amendment perspective, Judy should first ask Billy to turn over the clippers. If Billy refuses, Judy probably has enough information to initiate a search, based primarily on Mr. Travis's eyewitness account of the clippers. Judy should begin the search with Billy's backpack or other carryall before searching Billy directly. Also, it is important for Judy to only search those places it is reasonable to believe that the clippers can be found. Lastly, Judy's search should not be overly intrusive given the fact that she is looking for fingernail clippers and not something more dangerous.

Principal Judy should also know the policies and procedures of the school and district. A "reasonable administrator" in this case is responsible for knowing the district's weapons policy and the school's disciplinary protocol. (And in this case, knowing the policies and procedures certainly includes being aware of Billy's IEP needs.) Failure to know and correctly determine if the nail clippers fall within the category of a weapon and failure to know the disciplinary procedures and consequences associated with this matter could lead to personal liability against Judy.

Another important element of this case is the due process provided to each student. Here it is important for the principal to give each student—individually—an uninterrupted chance to tell his side of the story. Not only will this help the principal better ascertain the facts, but if either student is suspended for his actions, an uninterrupted opportunity to respond to the allegations is required.

In contacting each student's parent or guardian, it is critical to maintain student privacy rights as guaranteed by

. For example, when contacting Billy's grandmother, Principal Judy should only discuss Billy and his role in the altercation. If the grandmother asks who else was involved in the argument, Principal Judy should not reveal Rafael's name or his role in the situation. If Billy wants to tell his grandmother all about Rafael that evening, that's fine; however, these details should not come from school officials.

Also important to this situation is the fact that Billy and Rafael are minority students whose parents or guardians may have a primary language other than English. If this is the case, it is critical that Principal Judy is able to communicate with each parent or guardian in a language and manner in which he or she feels comfortable. If Judy is unable to communicate effectively, an interpreter should be found. In this case, it is probably not a good idea to have the student serve in this capacity. Any notices that are sent home regarding this situation should—whenever possible—be written in a language in which the parent or guardian is fluent.

Lastly, documentation is the key to successfully handling this situation. Should this matter to be appealed to the school board or a court of law, good documentation is key in helping the lawyers successfully resolve the matter. From practical experience, I can tell you that well-written statements from the teacher, any witnesses, and the investigating administrator are critical. The last place that I want to be learning about the facts of the case is with the parties taking a deposition or appearing on the witness stand. From a lawyer's perspective, I want to see statements prepared within a reasonable time frame after the incident, when the parties clearly remember the details. This is often the difference between being able to get the case dismissed and proceeding with time-consuming and potentially expensive litigation.

Biographies

Jim Burgett

Jim Burgett has served as a teacher, principal, and superintendent at the elementary, middle, and high school levels. He was named Illinois Superintendent of the Year and Illinois Administrator of the Year. Throughout his career, he has won many awards for his leadership and service to both education and to his communities. The districts that Jim has led have also been the recipients of many national awards, including the Blue Ribbon Award. Jim also implemented a plan that has resulted in 25 teachers becoming Nationally Board Certified.

Jim speaks and provides professional development to audiences throughout the United States and has previously written three published books: ***What Every Superintendent and Principal Needs to Know, The Perfect School,*** and ***Teachers Change Lives 24/7.*** Consulting, strategic plan development, and training teachers, administrators, and board members are a few of the services that Jim provides on a regular basis.

Jim holds three degrees in teaching and administration and is a lead provider of administrative academy development and implementation. He passionately strives to make a difference for kids through his teaching, speaking, and written words.

What makes Jim Burgett unique and in such demand is his ability to access a situation and offer practical and meaningful insights. His proven leadership and ability to inspire have made him an "in demand" author, speaker, and educational leader.

Brian D. Schwartz

Brian Schwartz has practiced law for fifteen years and has concentrated his practice in education law for the last eleven years. Brian strives to provide his clients with sound, practical legal advice that is geared toward solving problems, not creating them.

In addition to maintaining an active private practice, Brian serves as the associate director and general counsel to the Illinois Principals Association. He is also an adjunct professor at the University of Illinois at Springfield where he teaches several undergraduate and graduate courses on school and employment law. Previously, Brian served as an administrative hearing officer and special prosecutor for the Illinois Secretary of State.

Brian is the author of ***The Law of Homeschooling***, published in 2008. He has also written numerous book chapters, law review articles, and scholarly publications. Brian is a popular speaker and presenter and has spoken nationally and internationally on issues pertaining to school law.

Brian previously served on the national board of directors of the Education Law Association and is the past chair of the Illinois State Bar Association's Education Law Section Council. He is member of the Illinois and National Council of School Attorneys.

Brian lives in Springfield, Illinois, with his wife, Jennifer, who is an elementary school administrator. They have two children, four cats, and a dog.

Comments?

We would love to hear from you. If you have questions, comments, thoughts, ideas, or just want to share, please feel free to contact us:

Brian Schwartz: edlawyer@comcast.net

Jim Burgett: jburgett@burgettgroup.com

Index

Table of Cases

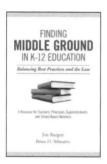